The Disuniting
of America

☆ ☆ ☆ ☆

Books by

ARTHUR M. SCHLESINGER, JR.

ORESTES A. BROWNSON

THE AGE OF JACKSON

THE VITAL CENTER

THE GENERAL AND THE PRESIDENT
(with Richard Rovere)

THE CRISIS OF THE OLD ORDER

THE COMING OF THE NEW DEAL

THE POLITICS OF UPHEAVAL

THE POLITICS OF HOPE

A THOUSAND DAYS: JOHN F. KENNEDY IN THE WHITE
HOUSE

THE BITTER HERITAGE

THE CRISIS OF CONFIDENCE

THE IMPERIAL PRESIDENCY

ROBERT KENNEDY AND HIS TIMES

THE CYCLES OF AMERICAN HISTORY

The Disuniting of America

Reflections on a
Multicultural Society

☆ ☆ ☆ ☆

Revised and Enlarged Edition

ARTHUR M. SCHLESINGER, JR.

W · W · NORTON & COMPANY

New York London

This book was first published by Whittle Books as part of The Larger
Agenda Series. Reprinted by arrangement with Whittle
Communications, L.P

For information about permission to reproduce selections from this book,
write to Permissions, W. W. Norton & Company, Inc., 500 Fifth Avenue,
New York, NY 10110.

The text of this book is composed in Caledonia with the display set in
Caledonia. Composition and manufacturing by the Haddon Craftsmen,
Inc.

Library of Congress Cataloging-in-Publication Data
Schlesinger, Arthur Meier, 1917–
The disuniting of America : reflections on a multicultural society
/ Arthur M. Schlesinger, Jr. —Rev. and enlarged ed.
p.   cm.
Includes bibliographical references (p.   ) and index.
ISBN 0-393-04580-3
1. United States—Ethnic relations.   2. United States—
Civilization.   3. Pluralism (Social sciences)—United States.
4. Multicultural education—United States.   I. Title.
E184.A1S34   1998
973—dc21   97-25124
CIP

W. W. Norton & Company, Inc., 500 Fifth Avenue, New York, N.Y. 10110
http://www.wwnorton.com

W. W. Norton & Company Ltd., 10 Coptic Street, London WC1A 1PU

1 2 3 4 5 6 7 8 9 0

Contents

☆ ☆ ☆ ☆

Foreword

to the Second Edition

The Disuniting of America was first published in 1991 by Whittle Books in its Larger Agenda Series as a contribution to the debate over the then new phenomenon of "multiculturalism." In 1992 W. W. Norton brought out a slightly revised trade edition.

In the half dozen years since original publication, new aspects of the debate have emerged. This second Norton edition brings the text up to date, amplifies a number of points, identifies new issues, and adds an epilogue discussing the impact on the Bill of Rights of both multiculturalism on the left and monoculturalism on the right. A new appendix contains the author's annotated list of books that indispensably illuminate the American experience.

Arthur M. Schlesinger, Jr.

Foreword

☆ ☆ ☆ ☆

The fading away of the cold war has brought an era of ideological conflict to an end. But it has not, as forecast, brought an end to history. One set of hatreds gives way to the next. Lifting the lid of ideological repression in eastern Europe releases ethnic antagonisms deeply rooted in experience and in memory. The disappearance of ideological competition in the third world removes superpower restraints on national and tribal confrontations. As the era of ideological conflict subsides, humanity enters—or, more precisely, re-enters—a possibly more dangerous era of ethnic and racial animosity.

The hostility of one tribe for another is among the most instinctive human reactions. Yet the history of our planet has been in great part the history of the mixing of peoples. Mass migrations have produced mass animosities from the beginning of time. Today, as the twentieth century draws to an end, a number of factors—not just the evaporation of the cold war but, more profoundly, the development of swifter modes of communication and transport, the acceleration of population growth, the breakdown of traditional social structures, the flight from tyranny, from poverty, from famine, from ecological disaster, the dream of a better life somewhere else—converge to drive people across national frontiers.

The world shrinks, and its population is more mixed up today than ever before. Shrinkage subjects the world to a whipsaw, tearing it in opposite directions—intense pressures toward globalization on the one hand, toward fragmentation on the other. The world market, electronic technologies, instantaneous communications, e-mail, CNN—all undermine the nation-state and develop a world without frontiers. At the same time, these very internationalizing forces drive ordinary people to seek refuge from unrelenting global currents beyond their control and understanding. The more people feel themselves adrift in a vast, impersonal, anonymous sea, the more desperately they swim toward any familiar, intelligible, protective life-raft; the more they crave a politics of identity. Integration and disintegration thus are the opposites that feed on one another. The more the world integrates, the more people cling to their own in groups increasingly defined in these post-ideological days by ethnic and religious loyalties.

What happens when people of different ethnic origins, speaking different languages and professing different religions, settle in the same geographical locality and live under the same political sovereignty? Unless a common purpose binds them together, tribal antagonisms will drive them apart. In the century darkly ahead, civilization faces a critical question: *What is it that holds a nation together?*

No one in the nineteenth century thought more carefully about representative government than John Stuart Mill. The two elements that defined a nation, as Mill saw it, were the desire on the part of the inhabitants to be governed together and the "common sympathy" instilled by shared history, values, and language. "Free institutions," he wrote, "are next to impossible in a country made up of different nationalities. Among a people without fellow feeling, especially if they read and speak different languages, the united public opinion, necessary to the working of representative government, cannot exist. . . . It is in general a necessary condition of free institutions that the boundaries of government should coincide in the main with those of nationalities."

In our world, those boundaries coincide less and less. There are few ethnically homogeneous states left. Events each day demonstrate the fragility of national cohesion. Everywhere you look, tribalism is the cause of the breaking of nations. The Soviet Union, Yugoslavia, Czechoslovakia have already split. India, Indonesia, Ireland, Israel, Lebanon, Sri Lanka, Afghanistan, Rwanda are in ethnic or religious turmoil. Ethnic tensions disturb and divide China, South Africa, Romania, Turkey, Georgia, Azerbaijan, the Philippines, Ethiopia, Somalia, Nigeria, Liberia, Angola, Sudan, Congo, Guyana, Trinidad—you name it. Even nations as stable and civilized as Britain and France, Belgium, and Spain, face rising ethnic and racial troubles. "The virus of tribalism," says the *Economist,* ". . . risks becoming the AIDS of international politics—lying dormant for years, then flaring up to destroy countries."

Take the case of our neighbor to the north. Canada has long been considered the most sensible and placid of nations. "Rich, peaceful and, by the standards of almost anywhere else, enviably successful," the *Economist* observes: yet today "on the brink of bust-up." Michael Ignatieff (the English-resident son of a Russian-born Canadian diplomat and thus an example of the modern mixing of peoples) writes of Canada, "Here we have one of the five richest nations on earth, a country so uniquely blessed with space and opportunity that the world's poor are beating at the door to get in, and it is tearing itself apart. . . . If one of the top five developed nations on earth can't make a federal, multi-ethnic state work, who else can?"

The answer to that increasingly vital question has been, at least until recently, the United States.

Now how have Americans succeeded in pulling off this almost unprecedented trick? Countries break up when they fail to give ethnically diverse peoples compelling reasons to see themselves as part of the same nation. As Chinua Achebe, the Nigerian novelist, writes of his own country, one of the richest in Africa but today on the brink of chaos, "This is the Nigerians' greatest weakness—their inability to face grave threats as one people instead of as competing religious and ethnic interests."

The United States has worked, thus far. A multiethnic country, it has somehow, except for a terrible civil war, cohered and endured. What is it that, in the absence of a common ethnic origin, has kept Americans together over two turbulent centuries? For America was multiethnic from the start. Hector St. John de Crèvecoeur emigrated from France to the American colonies in 1759, married an American woman, settled on a farm in Orange County, New York, and published his *Letters from an American Farmer* during the American Revolution. This eighteenth-century French American marveled at the astonishing diversity of the other settlers—"a mixture of English, Scotch, Irish, French, Dutch, Germans, and Swedes," a "strange mixture of blood" that you could find in no other country.

He recalled one family whose grandfather was English, whose wife was Dutch, whose son married a French-woman, and whose present four sons had married women of different nationalities. "From this promiscuous breed," he wrote, "that race now called Americans have arisen." (The word *race* as used in the eighteenth and nineteenth centuries meant what we mean by nationality today; thus people spoke of "the English race," "the German race," and so on.) What, Crèvecoeur mused, were the characteristics of this suddenly emergent American race? *Letters from an American Farmer* propounded a famous question: "What then is the American, this new man?" (Twentieth-century readers must overlook eighteenth-century male obliviousness to the existence of women.)

Crèvecoeur gave his own question its classic answer: *"He* is an American, who leaving behind him all his ancient prejudices and manners, receives new ones from the new mode of life he has embraced, the new government he obeys, and the new rank he holds. The American is a new man, who acts upon new principles. . . . *Here individuals of all nations are melted into a new race of men."*

The first great American historian soon reinforced Crèvecoeur's point. "Annihilate the past of any one leading nation of the world," George Bancroft wrote,

and our destiny would have been changed. Italy and Spain, in the persons of Columbus and Isabella, joined together for the great discovery that opened America to emigration and commerce; France contributed to its independence; the search for the origin of the language we speak carries us to India; our religion is from Palestine; of the hymns sung in our churches, some were first heard in Italy, some in the deserts of Arabia, some on the banks of the Euphrates; our arts come from Greece; our jurisprudence from Rome; our maritime code from Russia; England taught us the system of Representative Government; the noble Republic of the United Provinces [the Netherlands] bequeathed to us, in the world of thought, the great idea of the toleration of all opinions; in the world of action, the prolific principle of federal union. Our country stands, therefore, more than any other, as the realisation of the unity of the race.

E pluribus unum: one out of many. The United States had a brilliant solution for the inherent fragility, the inherent combustibility, of a multiethnic society: the creation of a brand-new national identity by individuals who, in forsaking old loyalties and joining to make new lives, melted away ethnic differences—a national identity that absorbs and transcends the diverse ethnicities that come to our shore, ethnicities that enrich and reshape the common culture in the very act of entering into it.

` Those intrepid Europeans who had torn up their roots to brave the wild Atlantic *wanted* to forget a horrid past and to embrace a hopeful future. They *yearned* to become Americans. Their goals were escape, deliverance, assimilation. They saw America as a transforming nation, banishing dismal memories and developing a unique national character based on common political ideals and shared experiences. The point of America was not to preserve old cultures, but to produce a new *American* culture.

One reason why Canada, despite all its advantages, is so vulnerable to schism is that, as Canadians freely admit, their country lacks such a unique national identity. Attracted variously to Britain, France, and the United States, inclined for generous reasons to a policy of official multiculturalism, Canadians have never developed a strong sense of what it is to be a Canadian. As Sir John Macdonald, their first prime minister, put it, Canada has "too much geography and too little history."

The United States has had plenty of history. From the Revolution on, Americans have had a vigorous sense of national identity, forged in the War for Independence, articulated in the Declaration of 1776 and the Constitution of 1787, deepened by the subsequent experience of self-government. The power of the national creed accounts for our relative success in converting Crèvecoeur's "promiscuous breed" into one people and thereby making a multiethnic society work.

This is not to say that the United States has ever fulfilled Crèvecoeur's standard. New waves of immigration brought in people who fitted awkwardly into a society that was inescapably English in language, ideals, and institutions. For a long time the Anglo-Americans dominated American culture and politics and excluded those who arrived after them. Anglo-America did not easily assimilate immigrants from Ireland, from Germany, from southern and eastern Europe.

As for the nonwhite peoples—those long in America whom the European newcomers overran and massacred, or those others hauled in against their will from Africa and Asia—deeply bred racism put them all, red Americans, black Americans, yellow Americans, brown Americans, well outside the pale. We must face the shameful fact: historically America has been a racist nation. White Americans began as a people so arrogant in convictions of racial superiority that they felt licensed to kill red people, to enslave black people, and to import yellow and brown people for peon labor. We white Americans have been racist in our laws, in our institutions, in our customs, in our conditioned reflexes, in our souls. The curse of racism has been the great failure of the

American experiment, the glaring contradiction of American ideals and the still crippling disease of American life—"the world's fairest hope," wrote Herman Melville, "linked with man's foulest crime."

Yet even nonwhite Americans, miserably treated as they were, contributed to the formation of the national identity. They became members, if third-class members, of American society and helped give the common culture new form and flavor. The infusion of non-Anglo stocks and the experience of the New World steadily reconfigured the British legacy and made the United States, as we all know, a very different country today from Britain. As early as 1831, Alexis de Tocqueville, the great commentator on American democracy, was struck by "the immense difference between the English and their descendants in America."

The vision of America as melted into one people prevailed through most of the two centuries of the history of the United States. But the twentieth century has brought forth a new and opposing vision. One world war destroyed the old order of things and launched Woodrow Wilson's doctrine of the self-determination of peoples. Twenty years after, a second world war dissolved the western colonial empires and intensified ethnic and racial militancy around the planet. In the United States itself, new laws eased entry for immigrants from South America, Asia, and Africa and altered the composition of the American people.

In a nation marked by an even stranger mixture of blood than Crèvecoeur had known, his celebrated question is asked once more, with a new passion—and a new answer. Today many Americans disavow the historic goal of "a new race of man." The escape from origins yields to the search for roots. The "ancient prejudices and manners" disowned by Crèvecoeur have made a surprising comeback. A cult of ethnicity has arisen both among non-Anglo whites and among nonwhite minorities to denounce the goal of assimilation, to challenge the concept of "one people," and to protect, promote, and perpetuate separate ethnic and racial communities.

The eruption of ethnicity had many good consequences. The American culture began at last to give shamefully overdue recognition to the achievements of minorities subordinated and spurned during the high noon of Anglo dominance. American education began at last to acknowledge the existence and significance of the great swirling world beyond Europe. All this is to the good. Of course history should be taught from a variety of perspectives. Let our children try to imagine the arrival of Columbus from the viewpoint of those who met him as well as from those who sent him. Living on a shrinking planet, aspiring to global leadership, Americans must learn much more about other races, other cultures, other continents. As they do, they acquire a more complex and invigorating sense of the world—and of themselves.

But, pressed too far, the cult of ethnicity has had bad consequences too. The new ethnic gospel rejects the unifying vision of individuals from all nations melted into a new race. Its underlying philosophy is that America is not a nation of individuals at all but a nation of groups, that ethnicity is the defining experience for Americans, that ethnic ties are permanent and indelible, and that division into ethnic communities establishes the basic structure of American society and the basic meaning of American history.

Implicit in this philosophy is the classification of all Americans according to ethnic and racial criteria. But while the ethnic interpretation of American history, like the economic interpretation, is valid and illuminating up to a point, it is fatally misleading and wrong when presented as the whole picture. The ethnic interpretation, moreover, reverses the historic theory of America as one people—the theory that has thus far managed to keep American society whole.

Instead of a transformative nation with an identity all its own, America in this new light is seen as preservative of diverse alien identities. Instead of a nation composed of individuals making their own unhampered choices, America increasingly sees itself as composed of groups more or less ineradicable in their ethnic character. The multiethnic dogma abandons historic purposes, replacing assimilation by fragmentation, integration by separatism. It belittles *unum* and glorifies *pluribus*.

The historic idea of a unifying American identity is now in peril in many arenas—in our politics, our voluntary organizations, our churches, our language. And in no arena is the rejection of an overriding national identity more crucial than in our system of education.

Our schools and colleges train the citizens of the future. Our public schools in particular have been the primary instrument of assimilation and the primary means of forming an American identity. "The great melting-pot of America," said Woodrow Wilson, "the place where we are all made Americans of, is the public school, where men of every race and of every origin and of every station in life send their children, or ought to send their children, and where, being mixed together, the youngsters are all infused with the American spirit and developed into American men and American women." What students are taught in schools affects the way they will thereafter see and treat other Americans, the way they will thereafter conceive the purposes of the republic. The debate about the curriculum is a debate about what it means to be an American.

The militants of ethnicity contend that a main objective of public education should be the protection, strengthening, celebration, and perpetuation of ethnic origins and identities. Separatism, however, nourishes prejudices, magnifies differences, and stirs antagonisms. The consequent increase in ethnic and racial conflict lies behind the hullabaloo over "multiculturalism" and "political correctness," over the iniquities of the "Eurocentric" curriculum, and over the notion that history and literature should be taught not as intellectual disciplines but as therapies whose function is to raise minority self-esteem.

Watching ethnic conflict tear one nation after another apart, one cannot look with complacency at proposals to divide the United States into distinct and immutable ethnic and racial communities, each taught to cherish its own apartness from the rest. One wonders: Will the center hold? or will the melting pot give way to the Tower of Babel?

I don't want to sound apocalyptic about these developments. Education is always in ferment, and a good thing too. Schools and colleges have always been battlegrounds for debates over beliefs, philosophies, values.

The situation in our universities, I am confident, will soon right itself once the great silent majority of professors cry "enough" and challenge what they know to be voguish blather.

The impact of ethnic and racial pressures on our public schools is more troubling. The bonds of national cohesion are sufficiently fragile already. Public education should aim to strengthen those bonds, not to weaken them. If separatist tendencies go on unchecked, the result can only be the fragmentation, resegregation, and tribalization of American life.

I remain optimistic. My impression is that the historic forces driving toward "one people" have not lost their power. For most Americans this is still what the republic is all about. They resist extremes in the argument between "unity first" and "ethnicity first." "Most Americans," Governor Mario Cuomo has well said, "can understand both the need to recognize and encourage an enriched diversity as well as the need to ensure that such a broadened multicultural perspective leads to unity and an enriched sense of what being an American is, and not to a destructive factionalism that would tear us apart."

Whatever their self-appointed spokesmen may claim, most American-born members of minority groups, white or nonwhite, while they may cherish their heritages, still see themselves primarily as Americans and not primarily as Irish or Hungarians or Jews or Africans or Asians. A telling indicator is the rising rate of intermarriage across ethnic, religious, even (increasingly) racial lines. The belief in a unique American identity is far from dead.

But the burden to unify the country does not fall

primarily on the minorities. Assimilation and integration constitute a two-way street. Those who want to join America must be received and welcomed by those who already think they own America. Racism, as I have noted, has been the great national tragedy. In recent times white America has at last begun to confront the racism so deeply and shamefully inbred in our history. But the triumph over racism is incomplete. When old-line Americans, for example, treat people of other nationalities and races as if they were indigestible elements to be shunned and barred, they must not be surprised if minorities gather bitterly unto themselves and damn everybody else. Not only must *they* want assimilation and integration; *we* must want assimilation and integration too. The burden to make this a unified country lies more with the complacent majority than with the beleaguered minorities.

The American population has unquestionably grown more heterogeneous than ever in recent times. But this very heterogeneity makes the quest for unifying ideals and a common culture all the more urgent. America, Scott Fitzgerald said, is "a willingness of the heart." We have it within our power to make this a fair and a just land for all our people.

Recall the words of Mahatma Gandhi, once seen on public posters throughout India, a country far more fiercely divided than our own by ethnic and religious and linguistic and caste antagonisms. "We must cease," Gandhi said, "to be exclusive Hindus or Muslims or Sikhs, Parsis, Christians or Jews. Whilst we may staunchly adhere to our respective faiths, we must be Indians first and Indians last." It is because India has abandoned these teachings of Gandhi that it is so bitterly divided today.

In the spirit of Gandhi, while we heterogeneous Americans may staunchly adhere to our respective traditions and creeds, let us not forget that we are members one of another, Americans first and Americans last, tied together, in Martin Luther King's phrase, into "a single garment of destiny." In a world savagely rent by ethnic and racial antagonisms, it is all the more essential that the United States continue as an example of a how a highly differentiated society holds itself together.

Arthur M. Schlesinger, Jr.

The Disuniting
of America

☆ ☆ ☆ ☆

1

☆ ☆ ☆ ☆

"A New Race"?

At the beginning America was seen as a severing of roots, a liberation from the stifling past, an entry into a new life, an interweaving of separate ethnic strands into a new national design. "We have it in our power," said Thomas Paine for the revolutionary generation, "to begin the world all over again." The unstated national motto was "Never look back." "The Past is dead, and has no resurrection," wrote Herman Melville. ". . . The Past is the text-book of tyrants; the Future the Bible of the Free."

I

And the future was America—not so much a nation, Melville said, as a world. "You can not spill a drop of American blood without spilling the blood of the whole world. On this Western Hemisphere all tribes and people are forming into one federal whole." For Ralph Waldo Emerson too, like Crèvecoeur, like Melville, America was the distillation of the multifarious planet. As the burning of the temple at Corinth had melted and intermixed silver and gold to produce Corinthian brass, "a new compound more precious than any," so, Emerson wrote in his journal, in America, in this "asylum of all nations, the energy of Irish, Germans, Swedes, Poles, & Cossacks, & all the European tribes—of the Africans, & of the Polynesians, will construct a new race . . . as vigorous as the new Europe which came out of the smelting pot of the Dark Ages."

Melville was a novelist, Emerson an essayist; both were poets. George Washington was a sternly practical man. Yet he believed no less ardently in the doctrine of the "new race." "The bosom of America," Washington said, "is open . . . to the oppressed and persecuted of all Nations and Religions." But he counselled newcomers against retaining the "Language, habits and principles (good or bad) which they bring with them." Let them come not in clannish groups but as individuals, prepared for "intermixture with our people." Then they would be "assimilated to our customs, measures and laws: in a word, soon become *one people.*"

John Quincy Adams, another sternly practical man, similarly insisted on the distinctness of the new American identity. When a German baron contemplating emigration interviewed Adams as secretary of state, Adams admonished his visitor that emigrants had to make up their minds to one thing: *They must cast off the European skin, never to resume it. They must look forward to their posterity rather than backward to their ancestors."*

But how could Crèvecoeur's "promiscuous breed" be transformed into a "new race"? How was Emerson's "smelting pot" to fuse such disparate elements into Washington's "one people"? This question preoccupied another young Frenchman who arrived in America three quarters of a century after Crèvecoeur. "Imagine, my dear friend, if you can," Alexis de Tocqueville wrote back to France, "a society formed of all the nations of the world . . . people having different languages, beliefs, opinions: in a word, a society without roots, without memories, without prejudices, without routines, without common ideas, without a national character, yet a hundred times happier than our own." What alchemy could make this miscellany into a single society?

The answer, Tocqueville concluded, lay in the commitment of Americans to democracy and self-government. Civic participation, Tocqueville argued in *Democracy in America,* was the great educator and the great unifier.

How does it happen that in the United States, where the inhabitants have only recently immigrated to the land which they now occupy, and brought neither customs nor traditions

> with them there; where they met one another
> for the first time with no previous acquain-
> tance; where, in short, the instinctive love of
> country can scarcely exist; how does it happen
> that every one takes as zealous an interest in
> the affairs of his township, his country, and the
> whole state as if they were his own? It is be-
> cause everyone, in his sphere, takes an active
> part in the government of society.

Immigrants, Tocqueville said, become Americans
through the exercise of the political rights and civic re-
sponsibilities bestowed on them by the Declaration of
Independence and the Constitution.

And they became Americans in a more technical
sense because citizenship, at least for white America, was
defined not in the European style by *jus sanguinis*—law
of blood—but by an adaptation of *jus soli*—law of the
soil, i.e., of location. To become citizens, newcomers had
only to swear to support and defend the Constitution and
the laws of the land. In the words of Abraham Lincoln,
people who thus declared their allegiance, even though
not descended from the "iron men" who had won independence, were Americans "as though they were blood
of the blood and flesh of the flesh of the men who wrote
that Declaration." In the new republic civic commitment
replaced bloodlines as the test for citizenship.

Half a century after Tocqueville the next great foreign commentator on American democracy, James
Bryce, wrote *The American Commonwealth*. Immigration had vastly increased and diversified. Bryce's European friends expected that it would take a very long time

for America to assimilate these "heterogeneous elements." What struck Bryce, on the contrary, was what had struck Tocqueville: "the amazing solvent power which American institutions, habits, and ideas exercise upon newcomers of all races . . . quickly dissolving and assimilating the foreign bodies that are poured into her mass."

A century after Tocqueville, another foreign visitor, Gunnar Myrdal of Sweden, found the essence of the "solvent power" in what he called "the American Creed." Americans "of all national origins, regions, creeds, and colors," Myrdal wrote in 1944, hold in common "the *most explicitly expressed* system of general ideals" of any country in the West: the ideals of the essential dignity and equality of all human beings, of inalienable rights to freedom, justice, and opportunity.

The schools teach the principles of the Creed, Myrdal said; the churches preach them; the courts hand down judgments in their terms. Myrdal showed why the Creed held out hope even for those most brutally excluded by the white majority, the Creed acting as the spur forever goading white Americans to live up to their proclaimed principles, the Creed providing the legal structure that gives the wronged the means of fighting for their rights. "America," Myrdal said, "is continuously struggling for its soul."

II

The American Creed had its antecedents, and these antecedents lay primarily in a British inheritance as recast by a century and a half of colonial experience. How really new then was the "new race"? Crèvecoeur's vision implied an equal blending of European stocks, and Emerson's smelting pot generously added Cossacks, Africans, and Polynesians. In fact, the majority of the population of the 13 colonies and the weight of its culture came from Great Britain.

Having cleared most of North America of their French, Spanish, and Dutch rivals, the British were free to set the mold. The language of the new nation, its laws, its institutions, its political ideas, its literature, its customs, its precepts, its prayers, primarily derived from Britain. Crèvecoeur himself wrote his book not in his native French but in his acquired English. The "curse of Babel," Melville said, had been revoked in America, "and the language they shall speak shall be the language of Britain."

The smelting pot thus had, unmistakably and inescapably, an Anglocentric flavor. For better or worse, the white Anglo-Saxon Protestant tradition was for two centuries—and in crucial respects still is—the dominant influence on American culture and society. This tradition provided the standard to which other immigrant nationalities were expected to conform, the matrix into which they would be assimilated.

But as the nineteenth century proceeded, non-Anglo immigration gathered speed. European peasants who may never have dared go twenty miles from their birthplaces now undertook the unimaginable adventure of a journey across perilous seas to a strange land in search of a new life. The land was indeed strange; and they could not but feel a need for reassurance and security. So at first they tended to cling to their compatriots and to the language, schools, churches they brought with them. These ethnic enclaves served as staging areas for regrouping and basic training before entry was made into the larger and riskier American life.

These immigrants came principally from western and northern Europe. The Anglos often disliked the newcomers, disdained their uncouth presence, feared their alien religions and folkways. Germans and Scandinavians were regarded as clannish in their fidelity to the language and customs of the old country. The German fondness for beer gardens and jolly Sundays excited puritanical disapproval. The Irish were regarded as shiftless and drunken; moreover, they were papists, and their fealty to Rome, it was said, meant they could never become loyal Americans. They were subjected to severe discrimination in employment and were despised by genteel society. W. E. B. Du Bois, the black scholar, testified that when he grew up in Great Barrington, Massachusetts, in the 1870s, "the racial angle was more clearly defined against the Irish than against me."

As the flow of immigrants increased, so did resentment among the old-timers. By the 1850s immigrants made up half the population of New York and outnumbered native-born Americans in Chicago. Nativist organizations sprang up, like the Supreme Order of the Star-Spangled Banner and its political front, the American Party, calling for a lengthened naturalization process and curtailment of the political rights of the foreign-born. They were referred to as Know-Nothings because members of the Supreme Order, when asked about their secret oaths and rituals, would reply, "I know nothing."

In 1856 the Know-Nothings even ran a former president, Millard Fillmore, as their presidential candidate. "Our progress in degeneracy appears to me to be pretty rapid," observed Abraham Lincoln. "As a nation, we began by declaring that *all men are created equal.'* We now practically read it 'all men are created equal, *except negroes.'* When the Know-Nothings get control, it will read 'all men are created equal, except negroes, *and foreigners, and catholics.'* "

But the Know-Nothing party fell as quickly as it rose. In the century and a half since, despite recurrent xenophobic outbursts, no nativist political party has appeared to take its place. However prejudiced white Anglo-Saxons were in practice, they were ashamed to endorse nativism in principle. Equally important, an expanding economy in an underpopulated country required a steady influx of new hands. Immigration alleviated the labor shortage, and economic need overpowered moral and aesthetic repugnance.

The pre–Civil War immigrants steadily turned into Americans. "The frontier," in the words of its great historian, Frederick Jackson Turner, "promoted the formation of a composite nationality. . . . In the crucible of the frontier the immigrants were Americanized, liberated, and fused into a mixed race, English in neither nationality nor characteristics." In the crucible of the cities too assimilation proceeded apace. Even "the Irish immigrant's son," Bryce reported in 1888, "is an American citizen for all other purposes, even if he retain, which he seldom does, the hereditary Anglophobia."

III

After the Civil War came the so-called "new" immigration from southern and eastern Europe. Over 27 million arrived in the half-century from Lee's surrender at Appomattox to America's entry into the First World War— more than the total population of the country in 1850. The new immigrants—Italians, Poles, Hungarians, Czechs, Slovaks, Russians, Jews—settled mainly in the cities, where their bizarre customs, dress, languages, and religions excited new misgivings.

Yet the old faith in the power of Bryce's "amazing solvent" to fulfill Washington's conception of Americans as "one people" held fast. However much they suffered from social prejudice, the newcomers were not barred from civic participation, and civic participation indoctrinated them in the fundamentals of the American Creed. They altered the ethnic composition of the country, but they preserved the old ambition to become Americans.

The fastidious Henry James, revisiting his native land in 1904 after many years abroad, was at first dismayed by the alien bustle of Ellis Island. But he soon understood and appreciated "the ceaseless process of the recruiting of our race, of the plenishing of our huge national *pot-au-feu,* of the introduction of fresh . . . foreign matter into our heterogeneous system." Though he wondered at times what immigration would do to Americans "ethnically, and thereby physiognomically, linguistically, *personally,*" though he saw at times "the 'ethnic' apparition" sitting like a skeleton at the feast, he was more impressed by the "colossal" machinery that so efficiently converted the children of immigrants into Americans—the political and social habit, the common school, the newspaper, all so reliably producing what James called "the 'ethnic" synthesis." He spoke with something like awe about "the cauldron of the 'American' character."

New race, one people, smelting pot, *pot-au-feu,* cauldron—the original faith received its most celebrated metaphor a few years after James's visitation. In 1908 a play by Israel Zangwill, an English writer of Russian Jewish origin, opened in Washington. *The Melting-Pot* tells the story of a young Russian Jewish composer in New York. David Quixano's artistic ambition is to write a symphony expressing the vast, harmonious interweaving of races in America, and his personal hope is to overcome racial barriers and marry Vera, a beautiful Christian girl. "America," David cries, "is God's crucible, the great Melting-Pot where all the races of Europe are melting and reforming! . . . Here you stand in your fifty groups, with your fifty languages . . . and your fifty blood hatreds. . . . A fig for your feuds and vendettas! Germans and Frenchmen, Irishmen and Englishmen, Jews and Russians—into the Crucible with you all! God is making the American."

The climactic scene takes place on the roof garden of a lower-Manhattan settlement house. In the background the Statue of Liberty gleams in the sunset. The composer, alone with Vera, gestures toward the city:

There she lies, the great Melting-Pot—listen!
Can't you hear the roaring and the bubbling?
Ah, what a stirring and a seething! Celt and

Latin, Slav and Teuton, Greek and Syrian,—
black and yellow—

VERA (*softly nestling to him*): Jew and Gentile—

DAVID: Yes, East and West, and North and South, the palm and the pine, the pole and the equator, the crescent and the cross. . . . Here shall they all unite to build the Republic of Man and the Kingdom of God. Ah, Vera, what is the glory of Rome and Jerusalem where all nations and races come to worship and look back, compared with the glory of America, where all races and nations come to labour and look forward! . . . (*Far back, like a lonely, guiding star, twinkles over the darkening water the torch of the Statue of Liberty. From below comes up the softened sound of voices and instruments joining in 'My Country, 'tis of Thee.' The curtain falls slowly.*)

When the curtain fell in Washington and the author walked onstage, President Theodore Roosevelt called from his box: "That's a great play, Mr. Zangwill, that's a great play." "I'm not a Bernard Shaw man or Ibsen man, Mrs. Zangwill," T. R. later told the playwright's wife. "No, *this* is the stuff." Zangwill subsequently dedicated the printed play to Roosevelt. *The Melting-Pot* played before rapt audiences across the country. Jane Addams of Hull-House in Chicago observed that Zangwill had performed "a great service to America by reminding us of the high hopes of the founders of the Republic."

IV

Yet even as audiences cheered *The Melting-Pot*, Zangwill's metaphor raised doubts. One had only to stroll around the great cities, as Basil March did in William Dean Howells's *A Hazard of New Fortunes*, to see that the melting process was incomplete. Ethnic minorities were forming their own *quartiers* in which they lived in their own way—not quite that of the lands they had left but not that of Anglocentric America either: Little Italy, Chinatown, Yorkville, Harlem, and so on.

Nor was the WASP culture showing great inclination to ease their access into Anglo-America. And when it did, when barriers fell, when new immigrants gained acceptance through money or celebrity, there loomed the prospect of intermarriage. In having his drama turn on marriage between people of different races and religions, Zangwill, who had himself married a Christian, emphasized where the melting pot must inexorably lead: to the submergence of separate ethnic identities in the new American race.

Was such a result desirable? Many immigrants doubtless thought so. In the early twentieth century, most of their children certainly did. But soon ethnic spokesmen began to appear, moved by real concern for distinctive ethnic values and also by real if unconscious vested interest in the preservation of ethnic constituencies. Jewish reviewers castigated Zangwill: "All the worse for you and me, brother," wrote one, "who are to be cast into and dissolved in the crucible." Even some of Anglo-

Saxon descent deplored the obliteration of picturesque foreign strains for the sake of insipid Anglocentric conformity.

The impression grew that the melting pot was a device to impose Anglocentric images and values upon hapless immigrants—an impression reinforced by the rise of the "Americanization" movement in response to the new polyglot immigration. Americanization programs, benign in intent, sought to expedite assimilation by offering immigrants special education in language, citizenship, and American history. The outbreak of war in 1914 gave Americanization a more coercive edge. Even presidents as friendly to immigrants as Theodore Roosevelt and Woodrow Wilson worried whether in crisis "hyphenated" Americans might not be more loyal to the old country than to their adopted land.

Three days after a German submarine sank the *Lusitania,* Wilson addressed an audience of recently naturalized citizens in Philadelphia. "You cannot become thorough Americans," he told them, "if you think of yourselves in groups. America does not consist of groups. A man who thinks of himself as belonging to a particular national group in America has not yet become an American."

"We can have no 'fifty-fifty' allegiance in this country," Theodore Roosevelt said two years later. "Either a man is an American and nothing else, or he is not an American at all." He condemned Americans who saw the world from the standpoint of another nation. "We Americans are children of the crucible," T. R. said. "The crucible does not do its work unless it turns out those cast into it in one national mould."

V

"One national mould"? Not everyone agreed. In 1915 Horace Kallen, a Jewish-American philosopher, wrote an essay for *The Nation* entitled "Democracy Versus the Melting-Pot." The melting pot, Kallen argued, was valid neither as a fact nor as an ideal. What impressed him was, on the contrary, the persistence of ethnic groups and their distinctive traditions. Unlike freely chosen affiliations, Kallen said, the ethnic bond was both involuntary and immutable. "Men may change their clothes, their politics, their wives, their religions, their philosophies, to a greater or lesser extent: they cannot change their grandfathers. Jews or Poles or Anglo-Saxons, in order to cease being Jews or Poles or Anglo-Saxons, would have to cease to be."

Ethnic diversity, Kallen observed, enriches American civilization. He saw the nation not as one people, except in a political and administrative sense, but rather "as a federation or commonwealth of national cultures . . . a democracy of nationalities, cooperating voluntarily and autonomously through common institutions . . . a multiplicity in a unity, an orchestration of mankind." This conception he came to call "cultural pluralism."

Kallen was unclear on the question of how to encourage ethnic separatism without weakening the original ideal of a single society. One critic warned that cultural pluralism would "result in the Balkanization of these United States." But Kallen made his attack on Anglo-centered assimilation at a time when critics of the melting pot could reasonably assume the solidity of the overarching framework. Because he considered political unity a given, he put his emphasis on the protection of cultural diversity.

Cultural pluralism was at first a minority gospel, confined to academics, intellectuals, and artists. The larger public in the postwar years experienced disenchantment with Europe, a Red Scare directed largely against aliens, the rise of the anti-Catholic Ku Klux Klan, and a campaign, realized in the Immigration Act of 1924, to freeze the ethnic composition of the American people. The new law established quotas on the basis of the national origins of the population in 1890, thereby drastically reducing the flow from southern and eastern Europe.

The xenophobic nationalism of the 1920s was followed in the 1930s by crises that, on some levels divisive, nevertheless strengthened the feeling that all Americans were in the same boat and had better pull together. The Great Depression and the Second World War showed the desperate necessity of national cohesion within the frame of shared national ideals. "The principle on which this country was founded and by which it has always been governed," Franklin D. Roosevelt said in 1943, "is that Americanism is a matter of the mind and heart; Americanism is not, and never was, a matter of race and ancestry. A good American is one who is loyal to this country and to our creed of liberty and democracy."

VI

Gunnar Myrdal in 1944 showed no hesitation in declaring the American Creed the common possession of all Americans, even as his great book *An American Dilemma* provided a magistral analysis of America's most conspicuous betrayal of the Creed: the treatment by white Americans of black America.

Noble ideals had been pronounced as if for all Americans, yet in practice they applied only to white people. Most interpretations of the national identity from Crèvecoeur on were for whites only. Even Horace Kallen, the champion of cultural pluralism, made no provision in his "democracy of nationalities" for black or red or brown or yellow Americans.

Tocqueville was an exception in factoring persons of color into the American equation. With his usual prescience, he identified racism as the irremediable flaw in American democracy. This "most grasping nation on the globe" had doomed the red man to extinction; and the presence of a black population was "the most formidable of all the ills that threaten the future of the Union." The more optimistic Emerson and Zangwill had thrown nonwhite nationalities into their smelting or melting pots, but Tocqueville saw racist exclusion as deeply ingrained in the national character.

History supported this judgment. White settlers had systematically pushed the American Indians back, killed their braves, seized their lands, and sequestered their tribes. They had brought Africans to America to work their plantations and Chinese to build their railroads. They had enunciated glittering generalities of freedom and withheld them from people of color. Their Constitution protected slavery, and their laws made distinctions on the basis of race. Though they eventually emancipated the slaves, they conspired in the reduction of the freedmen to third-class citizenship. Their Chinese Exclusion acts culminated in the total prohibition of Asian immigration in the Immigration Act of 1924. It occurred to damned few white Americans in these years that Americans of color were also entitled to the rights and liberties promised by the Constitution.

Yet what Bryce had called "the amazing solvent power" of American institutions and ideas retained its force, even among those most cruelly oppressed and excluded. Myrdal's polls of Afro-America showed the "determination" of blacks "to hold to the American Creed." Ralph Bunche, one of Myrdal's collaborators, observed that every man in the street—black, red, and yellow as well as white—regarded America as the "land of the free" and the "cradle of liberty." The American Creed, Myrdal surmised, meant even more to blacks than to whites, since it was the great means of claiming their unfulfilled rights. Blacks, new immigrants, Jews, and other disadvantaged groups, Myrdal said, "could not possibly have invented a system of political ideals which better corresponded to their interests."

The Second World War gave the Creed new bite. Hitler's racism forced Americans to look hard at their own racial assumptions. How, in fighting against Hitler's doctrine of the Master Race abroad, could Americans maintain a doctrine of white supremacy at home? How, with China a faithful American ally, could Americans continue to forbid Chinese to become American citizens? If the war did not end American racism, at least it drove much racial bigotry underground. The rethinking of racial issues challenged the conscience of the majority and raised the consciousness of minorities.

Emboldened by the Creed, blacks organized for equal opportunities in employment, opposed segregation in the armed forces, and fought in their own units on many fronts. After the war, the civil rights revolution, so long deferred, accelerated black self-reliance. So did the collapse of white colonialism around the world and the appearance of independent black states.

Across America minorities proclaimed their pride and demanded their rights. Women, the one "minority" that in America constituted a numerical majority, sought political and economic equality. Jews gained new solidarity from the Holocaust and then from the establishment of a Jewish state in Israel. Changes in the immigration law dramatically increased the numbers arriving from Hispanic and Asian lands, and, following the general example, they asserted their own prerogatives. American Indians mobilized to reclaim rights and lands long since appropriated by the white man; their spokesmen even rejected the historic designation in which Indians had taken deserved pride and renamed themselves Native Americans.

The civil rights revolution provoked new declarations of ethnic identity by the now long-resident "new migration" from southern and eastern Europe—Italians, Greeks, Poles, Czechs, Slovaks, Hungarians. Claiming to speak for white minorities aggrieved by the idea of the

melting pot, Michael Novak, an early and influential the-
orist of multiculturalism, wrote *The Rise of the Unmeltable Ethnics.* "Growing up in America," Novak said,
"has been an assault upon my sense of worthiness," and
to improve his self-esteem he affirmed the need for a
politics of identity. Against the conception of America as
a nation of individuals, Novak hailed what he called "the
new ethnic politics," which, he said, "asserts that *groups*
can structure the rules and goals and procedures of
American life."

The passion for "roots" was reinforced by the "third-
generation" effect formulated in Hansen's Law, named
after Marcus Lee Hansen, the great pioneer in immigration history: "What the son wishes to forget the grandson
wishes to remember." It was reinforced too, and powerfully, by the waning American optimism about the nation's prospects. For two centuries Americans had been
confident that life would be better for their children than
it was for them. In their exuberant youth, Americans had
disdained the past and, as John Quincy Adams urged,
looked forward to their posterity rather than backward to
their ancestors. Amid forebodings of national decline,
Americans now began to look forward less and backward
more. The rising cult of ethnicity was a symptom of de-
creasing confidence in the American future.

VII

Ethnic as a word has had a long history. It originally
meant "heathen" or "pagan" but soon came to mean anything pertaining to a race or nation. In this sense every-

one, even the Lowells and the Cabots, were ethnics. By the time Henry James used the word in *The American Scene,* however, "ethnic" had acquired an association with foreignness. As applied since the 1960s, it definitely means non-Anglo minorities—a reversion to the original sense of being beyond the pale.

The noun *ethnicity* meanwhile made its modern debut in 1940 in W. Lloyd Warner's Yankee City series. From its modest beginning in that sociological study, "ethnicity" moved vigorously to center stage in popular discourse. The bicentennial of American independence, the centennial of the Statue of Liberty, the restoration of Ellis Island—all turned from tributes to the melting pot into extravaganzas of ethnic distinctiveness.

The pressure for the new cult of ethnicity came less from the minorities en masse than from their often self-appointed spokesmen. Most ethnics, white and non-white, saw themselves primarily as Americans. "The cravings for 'historical identity,' " Gunnar Myrdal said at the height of the ethnic rage, "is not in any sense a people's movement. Those cravings have been raised by a few well-established intellectuals, professors, writers— mostly, I gather, of a third generation." Few of them, Myrdal thought, made much effort to talk to their own ethnic groups. This movement, Myrdal added with a certain contempt, was only "upper-class intellectual romanticism."

Still, ideologues, with sufficient publicity and time, could create audiences. Spokesmen with a vested interest in ethnic identification repudiated the ideal of assimilation. The melting pot, it was said, injured people by undermining their self-esteem. It denied them heroes—

"role models," in the jargon—from their own ethnic ancestries. Praise now went to Novak's "unmeltable ethnics."

In 1974, after testimony from ethnic spokesmen denouncing the melting pot as a conspiracy to homogenize America, Congress passed the Ethnic Heritage Studies Program Act—a statute that, by applying the ethnic ideology to all Americans, compromised the historic right of Americans to decide their ethnic identities for themselves. The act ignored those millions of Americans—surely a majority—who refused identification with any particular ethnic group.

The ethnic upsurge (it can hardly be called a revival because it was unprecedented) began as a gesture of protest against the Anglocentric culture. It became a cult, and today it threatens to become a counter-revolution against the original theory of America as "one people," a common culture, a single nation.

2

☆ ☆ ☆ ☆

History the Weapon

Writing history is an old and honorable profession with distinctive standards and purposes. The historian's goals are accuracy, analysis, and objectivity in the reconstruction of the past. But history is more than an academic discipline up there in the stratosphere. It also has its own role in the future of nations.

For history is to the nation rather as memory is to the individual. As an individual deprived of memory becomes disoriented and lost, not knowing where he has been or where he is going, so a nation denied a conception of its past will be disabled in dealing with its present and its future. As the means of defining national identity, history becomes a means of shaping history. The writing of history then turns from a meditation into a weapon. "Who controls the past controls the future," runs the Party slogan in George Orwell's *1984;* "who controls the present controls the past."

I

Historians do their damnedest to maintain the standards of their trade. Heaven knows how dismally we fall short of our ideals, how sadly our interpretations are dominated and distorted by unconscious preconceptions, how obsessions of race and nation blind us to our own bias. We remain creatures of our times, prisoners of our own experience, swayed hither and yon, like all sinful mortals, by partisanship, prejudice, dogma, by fear and by hope.

The spotlight we flash into the darkness of the past is guided by our own concerns in the present. When new preoccupations arise in our own times and lives, the spotlight shifts, throwing into sharp relief things that were always there but that earlier historians had casually excised from the collective memory. In this sense, the present may be said to re-create the past.

Historians must always strive toward the unattainable ideal of objectivity. But as we respond to contemporary urgencies, we sometimes exploit the past for nonhistorical purposes, taking from the past, or projecting upon it, what suits our own society or ideology. History thus manipulated becomes an instrument less of disinterested intellectual inquiry than of social cohesion and political purpose.

People live by their myths, and some may argue that the facts can be justifiably embroidered if embroiderment serves a higher good, such as the nurture of a nation or the elevation of a race. It may seem more important to maintain a beneficial fiction than to keep history pure—especially when there is no such thing as pure history anyway. This may have been what Plato had in mind when he proposed the idea of the "noble lie" in *The Republic.*

But enthusiasts are all too likely to confuse "noble lies" with reality. The corruption of history by nationalism is instructive. Nationalism remains, after two centuries, the most vital political emotion in the world—far more vital than social ideologies such as communism or fascism or even democracy. But it was not the product of spontaneous generation. "Nationalism is not the awakening of nations to self-consciousness," as Ernest Gellner has said; "it invents nations where they do not exist." Nationalism was developed by intellectuals in the interest of aspiring elites and thereafter propagated to receptive masses. And it continues to thrive because it taps potent emotions of history and locality to give individual lives meaning in an increasingly baffling universe.

Today the nationalist fever encircles the globe. In the West the contagion convulses Ireland and Israel, divides Belgium, Cyprus, and Canada, arouses Brittany, Corsica, and the Basque country. Nationalism broke up first the Soviet empire and then the Soviet Union itself. In the third world, nationalism, having overthrown Western colonialism, launches a horde of new states, large and micro, often at each other's throats in reenacting ancient quarrels of history.

Within nation-states, nationalism takes the form of ethnicity or tribalism. In country after country across the third world ethnic groups struggle for power and, in desperate cases, for survival. The ethnic upsurge in America, far from being unique, partakes of the global fever.

II

The invocation of history is indispensable to nations and groups in the process of making themselves. How else can a people establish the legitimacy of its personality, the continuity of its tradition, the correctness of its course?

Often history is invoked to justify the ruling class. "The past," writes the British historian J. H. Plumb, "has always been the handmaid of authority." This is top-dog history, designed to show how noble, virtuous, and inevitable existing power arrangements are. Because it vindicates the status quo and the methods by which power is achieved and maintained, it may be called exculpatory history.

Other times history is invoked to justify the victims of power, to vindicate those who reject the status quo. Isaiah Berlin has described how the "humiliated and defeated Germans" in the early nineteenth century lashed back against the arrogant French:

> They discovered in themselves qualities far superior to those of their tormentors. They con-

trasted their own deep, inner life of the spirit, their own profound humility, their selfless pursuit of true values—simple, noble, sublime— with the rich, worldly, successful, superficial, smooth, heartless, morally empty French. This mood rose to fever pitch during the national resistance to Napoleon, and was indeed the original exemplar of the reaction of many a backward, exploited, or at any rate patronised society, which, resentful of the apparent inferiority of its status, reacted by turning to real or imaginary triumphs and glories in its past, or enviable attributes of its own national or cultural character. . . . Hence the value of a real or imaginary rich historical past to inferiority-ridden peoples, for it promises, perhaps, an even more glorious future.

This is underdog history, designed to demonstrate what Bertrand Russell called the "superior virtue of the oppressed" by inventing or exaggerating past glories and purposes. It may be called compensatory history.

Both exculpatory and compensatory history use the past in order to shape the future. For 70 years in the Soviet Union, scholars practiced exculpatory history, sedulously defending every twist of the party line and every whim of the Kremlin dictatorship. Then came Gorbachev; and *glasnost* led in due course to the emancipation of historians.

For the first time ever, Russian historians became free to write honest history—to describe the purges and the gulags, to demythologize Stalin and even Lenin, to reassess Bukharin and even Trotsky, to condemn the Soviet-Nazi pact of 1939, to pronounce Stalin's U.S.S.R. a totalitarian state, even to doubt the sacred Revolution itself. "A new future requires a new past," said Eric Foner of Columbia after four months as a lecturer at Moscow State University. "To legitimize these far-reaching changes, the press and public officials now paint the history of the Soviet era in the blackest hues." As party-line history was an instrument of dictatorship, historical debate is an instrument of democracy.

In Japan the government in its dedication to exculpatory history rejected responsibility for aggressions and atrocities of half a century ago. School textbooks unrepentantly portray the Japanese conquest of Korea and invasion of China in terms so benevolent as to provoke official protests from Seoul and Beijing. Young Japanese are taught to see their country as a victim rather than the cause of the Pacific War.

When the eminent historian Professor Saburō Ienaga tried, as he wrote in the preface to the English edition of his notable book *The Pacific War*, "to show the Japanese people the naked realities," he was subjected to official persecution. Japanese courts upheld the Education Ministry's censorship of Ienaga's factual account of the Japanese "rape of Nanjing" in 1937. As Ienaga observed, the less the young people of Japan are taught the true history of the war, the greater the risk of a "similar danger" in years to come.

By the 1960s German historians had come to accept the crimes of Hitler as a unique German responsibility and to trace Nazism back to nineteenth-century German history and culture. But the revival of German nationalism in the 1980s set off a scholarly campaign to sanitize the national past. The crimes of Hitler, influential historians argued, were not unique, nor were they peculiarly German. All Hitler was doing was imitating genocidal policies invented by Stalin, substituting race for class. Hitler had no doubt done awful things, but other nations had committed comparable atrocities without suffering the same international disfavor. Nazism was deplorable but not fundamental, more a matter of bad luck and aberration.

As Franz Josef Strauss, the conservative leader, said, Germans must not let the vision of their glorious past "be blocked by the sight-screens of those accursed 12 years between 1933 and 1945. German history cannot be presented as an endless chain of mistakes and crimes." Michael Stürmer, a conservative historian, criticizes the German "obsession with their guilt" and calls for a new affirmation of national identity. Stürmer understands the stakes: "Loss of orientation and the search for identity are brothers. . . . Anyone who believes that this has no effect on politics and the future ignores the fact that *in a land without history, he who fills the memory, defines the concepts, and interprets the past, wins the future.*"

History is a weapon. Perhaps their own vicissitudes as a nation—from democracy to Nazism to communism back to democracy in half a century—have made Czechs particularly sensitive to the manipulations of history. "The first step in liquidating a people," a historian observes in Milan Kundera's *The Book of Laughter and Forgetting,* "is to erase its memory. Destroy its books, its culture, its history. Then have somebody write new books, manufacture a new culture, invent a new history.

Before long the nation will begin to forget what it is and what it was." "The struggle of man against power," says another character, "is the struggle of memory against forgetting."

Vaclav Havel, Czech playwright and president, made a pointed address in the presence of Kurt Waldheim of Austria. "He who fears facing his own past," Havel said, "must necessarily fear what lies before him. . . . Lying can never save us from the lie. Falsifiers of history do not safeguard freedom but imperil it. . . . Truth liberates man from fear." Honest history is the weapon of freedom.

III

American history was long written in the interests of white Anglo-Saxon Protestant males. My father, growing up in the 1890s in Xenia, a small Ohio town containing large contingents of Germans, Irish, and blacks, one day asked his father, who had come from Germany as a child and whose hero was Carl Schurz, the American general, politician, and reformer, why the schoolbooks portrayed England as the one and only mother country. My grandfather's wry comment was that apparently the only Germans worth mentioning were "the Hessians who had fought on the wrong side in the War for Independence." Irish and blacks fared even less well in schoolbooks, and the only good Indians were dead Indians. Non-WASPs were the invisible men (and women) in the American past.

The Anglocentric domination of schoolbooks was

based in part on unassailable facts. For better or for worse, American history has been shaped more than anything else by British tradition and culture. Like it or not, as Andrew Hacker, the Queens political scientist, puts it, "For almost all this nation's history, the major decisions have been made by white Christian men." To deny this perhaps lamentable but hardly disputable fact would be to falsify history. But history can also be falsified by suppression of uglier aspects of Anglo rule—callous discrimination against later immigrants, brutal racism against nonwhite minorities—and by the creation of filiopietistic myths.

Myth-making began as early as Parson Weems's biography of Washington. As Anglocentric myths grew, they were at times directed against the British themselves. Anglophobia died slowly in the United States; and, despite the current theory of a continuing Anglo-Saxon cultural conspiracy, American WASPs, from the Adamses in the eighteenth century to the Lodges in the twentieth, were always among the leading Anglophobes.

After the First World War, patriotic organizations, persuaded that Britain had tricked the United States into the struggle, hunted down pro-British propaganda in American textbooks—as 30 years later a new generation of superpatriots hunted down pro-Soviet propaganda. Scholars were charged with selling out to British gold and plotting to bring the republic back into the empire. Official investigations were launched against "Anglicized" books in New York City, Washington, D.C., St. Louis, and elsewhere. Wisconsin, Oklahoma, and Oregon passed "pure-history" laws.

William Hale Thompson, running for mayor of

Chicago in 1927 with the support of Colonel Mc-Cormick's Anglophobic *Chicago Tribune*, seized upon this agitation, promising to "biff King George on the snoot" if he dared come to Chicago. In his book *New Viewpoints in American History*, my father had an ironic sentence about the representatives of George V rendering homage "at the tomb of the great disloyalist and rebel of a former century, George Washington." Discovering *New Viewpoints* on a University of Chicago reading list, Big Bill Thompson denounced the "infamous book" and its infamous author for thus characterizing the sainted father of his country. A Thompson henchman, a Damon Runyon character called Sport Herrmann, tried to remove the "treason-tainted" book from the public library. Frustrated there, Sport bought himself a copy and burned it in a patriotic bonfire.

An early cultural pluralist, Big Bill Thompson was determined not only to "stop the defamation of America's heroes" but to see that justice was done to "heroes of Irish, Polish, German, Holland, Italian, and other extractions." As ruling groups cherish their set of self-justifying myths, so excluded groups seek counter-affirmations of their own historical and cultural dignity, myths celebrating, and often exaggerating in the manner so well described by Isaiah Berlin, their own unacknowledged contributions to the making of America.

IV

The ethnic enclaves thus developed a compensatory literature. Inspired by group resentment and pride, this

literature very often succumbed to the Platonic tempta-
tion of "noble lies." Professor John V. Kelleher, Harvard's
distinguished Irish-American scholar, provided gently
satiric testimony about the Irish case:

> My earliest acquaintance with Irish-American
> history of the written variety was gained from
> the sort of articles that used to appear in minor
> Catholic magazines or in the Boston Sunday
> papers. They were turgid little essays on the
> fact that the Continental Army was 76 percent
> Irish, or that many of George Washington's
> closest friends were nuns or priests, or that
> Lincoln got the major ideas for the Second In-
> augural Address from the Hon. Francis P.
> Mageghegan of Alpaca, New York, a pioneer
> manufacturer of cast-iron rosary beads.

This is what Professor Kelleher called the there's-always-
an-Irishman-at-the-bottom-of-it-doing-the-real-work approach to American history.

Such ethnic chauvinism was largely confined, however, to tribal celebrations. Even in Boston and environs,
where Irish pols dominated school and library boards,
they made no effort to impose their compensatory history
on the public-school curriculum. And as the Irish rose in
American society, Kelleher recalled, pietistic articles
began to vanish from the Boston press. "Now one is
rarely seen," he wrote in 1960, "even around March 17.
I wonder whose is the major component in the Conti-
nental Army these days." (The answer would probably be

blacks and Jews.) Kelleher was musing about the Irish in the spring of the year that an Irish Catholic was elected president of the United States—a signal of ultimate acceptance that relieved Irish-Americans of the need for ethnic cheerleading.

People from groups that began by sitting far beneath the salt may end, once they have made it themselves, by defending the Anglocentric canon. In 1990 Peggy Noonan, the charming and witty Irish-American ghostwriter for a second Irish-American president, urged that immigrants be instructed, not in the exploits of their own crowd, but in "the great unifying myths that define the dreams, characteristics, and special history of America." Otherwise, she said, "if our retelling of our past is dominated by the compulsive skepticism of the modern mind, with its ill-thought-out disdain, then we will stop being America."

Nor has anyone in recent years more wrathfully denounced scholarly iconoclasm than Professor Allan Bloom, the Jewish-American author of *The Closing of the American Mind.* "We are used to hearing the Founders charged with being racists, murderers of Indians, representatives of class interests," Professor Bloom wrote, condemning the debunkers for "weakening our convictions of the truth or superiority of American principles and our heroes."

Debunking is an ephemeral phenomenon, nothing to get excited about. If any kind of positive case can be made, rebunkers will appear in due course. The British historical journalist Paul Johnson can even make a hero out of Calvin Coolidge. History proceeds by revision and counterrevision. As the great Dutch historian Pieter Geyl splendidly put it, "History is indeed an argument without end."

V

The Irish and the Jews had their share of gristle in the American cauldron, but they finally made it: hence the emergence of people named Noonan and Bloom as defenders of Anglocentric verities. The situation is radically different for nonwhite minorities facing not snobbism but racism.

Most white Americans through most of American history simply considered colored Americans inferior and unassimilable. Not until the 1960s did integration become a widely accepted national objective. Even then, even after legal obstacles to integration fell, social, economic, and psychological obstacles remained. Blacks and Indians confront American democracy with its most tragic challenge.

Both black Americans and red Americans have every reason to seek redressment of the historical balance. Indians, however, lack the numbers, the unity, the visibility, and the political weight of African-Americans. Twelve percent of Americans are black, and the felt pressure to correct injustices of past scholarship comes mostly on their behalf. And indeed the cruelty with which white Americans have dealt with black Americans has been compounded by the callousness with which white historians have dealt with black history.

Even the best historians: Frederick Jackson Turner, dismissing the slavery question as a mere "incident" when American history is "rightly viewed"; Charles and Mary Beard in their famous *The Rise of American Civilization,* describing blacks as passive in slavery and ludicrous in Reconstruction and acknowledging only one black achievement—the invention of ragtime; Samuel Eliot Morison and Henry Steele Commager, writing about childlike and improvident Sambo on the old plantation. One can sympathize with W. E. B. Du Bois's rage after reading white histories of slavery and Reconstruction; he was, he wrote, "literally aghast at what American historians have done to this field . . . one of the most stupendous efforts the world ever saw to discredit human beings."

The job of redressing the balance has been splendidly undertaken in recent years by both white and black historians. Meticulous and convincing scholarship has reversed conventional judgments on slavery, on Reconstruction, on the role of the blacks in American life. After the murder of Medgar Evers in Mississippi in 1963, President Kennedy invited his widow and children to the White House. Later, Kennedy reflected on the days when Radical Republicans like Thaddeus Stevens advocated a tough Reconstruction policy toward the South. "I'm coming to believe that Thaddeus Stevens was right," he said. "I had always been taught to regard him as a man of vicious bias." He would not be taught that way today.

The reversal has extended from the world of scholarship to the popular culture. *Glory,* Edward Zwick's superb movie, told many white Americans for the first time about the record of black soldiers in the Civil War. How many had known before that 186,000 blacks served in the Union Army—about the same number as composed the entire United States Army in 1939?

But scholarly responsibility was only one factor behind the campaign of correction. History remains a weapon. "History's potency is mighty," Herbert Aptheker, the polemical chronicler of slave rebellions, has written. "The oppressed need it for identity and inspiration." (Aptheker, a devout Stalinist, was an old hand at the manipulation of history.) "The thing that has kept most of us, that is, African-Americans, almost crippled in this society," said Malcolm X, "has been our complete lack of knowledge concerning the past."

More than Irish or Italians or Jews, black Americans, after generations of psychological and cultural evisceration, have every right to seek an affirmative definition of their past. Far more than white ethnics, they perceive themselves to be in a trap of cultural "hegemony" in which they are flooded by white values and demeaning self-images. Whites, some black intellectuals argue, control "knowledge production," and the need is to overcome "communicentric hegemony"—that is, "a canon which reflects the hegemonic culture." For blacks the American dream has been pretty much of a nightmare, and, far more than white ethnics, they are driven by a desperate need to vindicate their own identity.

"The academic and social rescue and reconstruction of Black history," as Maulana Karenga put it in his influential *Introduction to Black Studies* ("a landmark in the intellectual history of African Americans," according to Molefi Kete Asante of Temple University), "is . . . [an]

indispensable part of the rescue and reconstruction of Black humanity. For history is the substance and mirror of a people's humanity in others' eyes as well as in their own eyes . . . not only what they have done, but also a reflection of who they are, what they can do, and equally important what they can become."

VI

One can hardly be surprised at the emergence of a there's-always-a-black-man-at-the-bottom-of-it-doing-the-real-work approach to American history. A man named Crispus Attucks led the mob that British troops fired upon in the Boston Massacre before the Revolution and was among those killed. He was a sailor and of dark complexion, perhaps a mulatto, perhaps an Indian. No one knows much about Crispus Attucks. But "to evaluate a book on Attucks solely by the canons of scholarly objectivity and historical accuracy is missing the point," one writer observes. "It ignores the necessity of creating black counterparts to the Nathan Hale and Molly Pitchers of the white past."

Why this necessity? "The extent to which the past of a people is regarded as praiseworthy," the white anthropologist Melville J. Herskovits wrote in his study of the African antecedents of American blacks, "their own self-esteem would be high and the opinion of others will be favorable." The failure to celebrate the past, black publicists say today—as British and Irish and Jewish publicists had said before them—is a powerful reason for low self-esteem in the present. The remedy is the recovery of bygone glories and heroes. "We've got to stop waiting for white folks to put us in their history books," says Professor Jacob Gordon of the University of Kansas. "The Jews have done a good job of this. We've got to create Afrocentric academies and create our own history books."

White domination of American schools and colleges, black academics say, results in Eurocentric, racist, elitist, imperialist indoctrination and in systematic denigration of black values and achievements. "Physical enslavement," notes Kofi Lomotey of the State University of New York in Buffalo, has been succeeded by "psychological enslavement." "In the public-school system," writes Felix Boateng of Eastern Washington University, "the orientation is so Eurocentric that white students take their identity for granted, and African-American students are totally deculturalized"—deculturalization being the "process by which the individual is deprived of his or her culture and then conditioned to other cultural values." White education, writes Maulana Karenga, cuts out blacks, "the fathers and mothers of humankind and human civilization," and aims to turn black students into "obscene caricatures of Europe, pathetic imitators of their oppressors." Liberation would be impossible "until the white monopoly on Black minds was broken." "In a sense," says Molefi Kete Asante, the Eurocentric curriculum is "killing our children, killing their minds."

In history, Western-civilization courses are seen as cultural imperialism designed to disparage non-Western traditions and to impress the Western stamp on people of all races. In literature, the "canon," the accepted list of essential books, is seen as an instrumentality of the white power structure. Nowhere can blacks discover adequate reflection or representation of the black self. Black students, one scholar writes, "succumb to a sort of brainwashing which denies them the ego-strength that comes from self-awareness, self-knowledge, and the security of group identity." Asante advises black students to take two sets of notes—one to help them pass the examinations, the other to preserve their sanity. "When they say Shakespeare was the greatest writer who ever lived, you write it down so you can pass the test. But you write in the margins, 'This is nonsense.' "

Some black educators even assert ultimate biological and mental differences, arguing that black students do not learn the way white students do and that the black mind works in a genetically distinctive way. Black children are said, in the jargon of the educationist, to "process information differently." "There are scientific studies that show, at early ages, the difference between Caucasian infants and African infants," says Clare Jacobs, a teacher in Washington, D.C. "Our African children are very expressive. Every thought we have has an emotional dimension to it, and Western education has historically subordinated the feelings." Charles Willie of Harvard finds several distinct "intelligences" of which the "communication and calculation" valued by whites constitute only two. Other kinds of "intelligence" are singing and dancing, in both of which blacks excel.

According to Professor Asa Hilliard, a black psychologist at Georgia State University, black students have cultural characteristics that whites lack: "high levels of energy, impulsive interrupting, and loud talking." (Hilliard's acquaintance with whites must be limited.) The "communication style" of the black child, writes another black psychologist, Na'im Akbar, includes considerable body language, eye movement, and positioning, "words that depend upon context for meaning and that have little meaning in themselves" and "a wide use of many coined interjections (sometimes profanity)."

To force black children to learn standard English, some contend, only deepens their sense of inferiority; blacks should therefore be taught in "black English"—street slang spoken in the inner city, later called Ebonics—as Hispanics should be taught in Spanish. The great Ebonics scare of 1996 dramatized this issue. The school board in Oakland, California, declared Ebonics "not a dialect of English" but a foreign language, entitling the Oakland schools to federal funds for programs designed to maintain a language's "legitimacy and richness." All this was rather like saying that cockney is a foreign language spoken by working-class Londoners.

Some professors even claimed West African origins for Ebonics, though a Nigerian journalist freshly arrived in the United States found Ebonics "totally unrecognizable, and those who argue that it has a West African origin are merely contriving a thesis to justify nonsense." The board quickly retreated under derision from blacks as well as whites. Even the Reverend Al Sharpton of New York, not known for restraint in racial matters, found the Oakland declaration "insulting" for implying that black kids were not up to learning standard English.

The Oakland board also argued that Ebonics was "genetically based." The Nigerian visitor observed, "It is certainly not in the African gene." It may be that the board meant only the genetic "family" to which, in linguistic terms, the language belonged. But others hold that the psychological difference between blacks and whites does have an organic base. Whites must strive for supremacy, according to the black psychiatrist Frances Cress, to make up for their racial inferiority, caused by their "genetic inability to produce the skin pigments of melanin which are responsible for all skin coloration." "Black superiority in the areas of mental development, neurological functioning, and psychomotor development," opines Amos Wilson, "[are] . . . all related to the possession of a high level of melanin."

Salvation lies in breaking the white, Eurocentric, racist grip on the curriculum and providing education that responds to colored races, colored histories, colored ways of learning and behaving. Europe has reigned long enough; it is the source of most of the evil in the world anyway; and the time is overdue to honor the African contributions to civilization so purposefully suppressed in Eurocentric curricula. Children from nonwhite minorities, so long persuaded of their inferiority by the white hegemons, need the support and inspiration that identification with role models of the same color will give them.

The answer, for some at least, is "Afrocentricity," described by Asante in his book of that title as "the centerpiece of human regeneration." There is, Asante contends, a single "African Cultural System." Wherever people of African descent are, "we respond to the same rhythms of the universe, the same cosmological sensibilities. . . . Our Africanity is our ultimate reality." Those who say that Africans and African-Americans have nothing in common but the color of their skin are talking nonsense. "There exists an emotional, cultural, psychological connection . . . that spans the ocean." Civilization originated in the highlands of East Africa, and "our ancestors do in fact gather to inspire us and do bring us victory."

VII

The belated recognition of the pluralistic character of American society has had a bracing impact on the teaching and writing of history. The women's-liberation movement, the civil rights movement, the ethnic upsurge, and other forms of group self-assertion force historians to look at old times in new ways. Scholars now explore such long-neglected fields as the history of women, of immigration, of blacks, Indians, Hispanics, homosexuals. Voices long silent ring out of the darkness of the past.

The result has been a reconstruction of American history partly on the merits and partly in response to gender and ethnic pressures. In 1987 the two states with both the greatest and the most diversified populations—California and New York—adopted new curricula for grades one to 12. Both state curricula materially increased the time allotted to non-European cultures.

The New York curriculum went further in minimizing Western traditions. A two-year global-studies course divided the world into seven regions—Africa, South Asia, East Asia, Latin America, the Middle East, Western Europe, and Eastern Europe—with each region given equal time. The history of Western Europe was cut back from a full year to one quarter of the second year. American history was reduced to a section on the Constitution; then a leap across Jefferson, Jackson, the Civil War, and Reconstruction to 1877.

In spite of the multiculturalization of the New York state history curriculum in 1987—a revision approved by such scholars as Eric Foner of Columbia and Christopher Lasch of Rochester—a newly appointed commissioner of education yielded to pressures from minority interests to consider still further revision. In 1989, a Task Force on Minorities: Equity and Excellence (not one historian among its 17 members) brought in a report, its first sentence sounding the keynote:

> African-Americans, Asian-Americans, Puerto Ricans/Latinos and Native Americans have all been the victims of an intellectual and educational oppression that has characterized the culture and institutions of the United States and the European American world for centuries.

The "systematic bias toward European culture and its derivatives," the report asserts, has "a terribly damaging effect on the psyche of young people of African, Asian, Latino, and Native American descent." The dominance of "the European-American monocultural perspective" explains why "large numbers of children of non-European descent are not doing as well as expected." The 1987 curriculum revision, the report concedes, did include more material on minority groups, but "merely adding marginal examples of 'other' cultures to an assumed dominant culture" cannot counteract "deeply rooted racist traditions"; all it produces is "Eurocentric multiculturalism."

Dr. Leonard Jeffries, the task force's consultant on African-American culture and a leading author of the report, discerns "deep-seated pathologies of racial hatred" even in the 1987 curriculum. A provocative teacher at the City College of New York, Jeffries describes Europeans as cold, individualistic, materialistic, and aggressive "ice people" who grew up in caves and have brought the world the three D's, "domination, destruction, and death," whereas Africans who grew up in sunlight, with the intellectual and physical superiority provided by melanin, are warm, humanistic, and communitarian "sun people." (He also tells his CCNY classes that "rich Jews" financed the slave trade.)

The consultant on Asian-American culture called for more pictures of Asian-Americans. The consultant on Latino culture found damning evidence of ethnocentric bias in such white usages as the Mexican War and the Spanish-American War. The ethnically correct designations should be the American-Mexican War and the Spanish-Cuban-American War. A later commentator objected to the term *slaves* on the ground that it "depersonalizes the oppression of a people. If a text were to use 'enslaved persons,' the act of enslavement would be made more explicit." The consultant on Native American culture wanted more space for Indians and bilingual education in Iroquois.

A new curriculum giving the four other cultures equitable treatment, the report concluded, would provide "children from Native American, Puerto Rican/Latino, Asian American, and African American cultures . . .

higher self-esteem and self-respect, while children from European cultures will have a less arrogant perspective."

The report views division into racial groups as the basic analytical framework for an understanding of American history. Its interest in history is not as an intellectual discipline but rather as social and psychological therapy whose primary purpose is to raise the self-esteem of children from minority groups. Nor does the report regard the Constitution or the American Creed as means of improvement. Jeffries scorns the Constitution, finding "something vulgar and revolting in glorifying a process that heaped undeserved rewards on a segment of the population while oppressing the majority." The belief in the unifying force of democratic ideals finds no echo in the report, no doubt because the ideals were disqualified by their Eurocentric origin. Indeed, the report takes no interest in the problem of holding a diverse republic together. Its impact is rather to sanction and deepen racial tensions.

VIII

The recent spread of Afrocentric programs to public schools represents an extension of the New York taskforce ideology. These programs are in most cases based on a series of "African-American Baseline Essays" conceived by the educational psychologist Asa Hilliard.

Hilliard's narration for the slide show "Free Your Mind, Return to the Source: The African Origin of Civilization" suggests his approach. "Africa," he writes, "is the mother of Western civilization"—an argument turning on the contention that Egypt was a black African country and the real source of the science and philosophy Western historians attribute to Greece. Africans, Hilliard continues, also invented birth control and carbon steel. They brought science, medicine, and the arts to Europe; indeed, many European artists, such as Browning and Beethoven, were in fact "Afro-European." They also discovered America long before Columbus, and the original name of the Atlantic Ocean was the Ethiopian Ocean.

Hilliard's African-American Baseline Essays were introduced into the school system of Portland, Oregon, in 1987. They have subsequently been the inspiration for Afrocentric curricula in Milwaukee, Indianapolis, Pittsburgh, Washington, D.C., Richmond, Atlanta, Philadelphia, Detroit, Baltimore, Camden, and other cities and continue at this writing to be urged on school boards and administrators anxious to do the right thing.

John Henrik Clarke's Baseline Essay on Social Studies begins with the proposition that "African scholars are the final authority on Africa." Egypt, he continues, "gave birth to what later became known as Western civilization, long before the greatness of Greece and Rome." "Great civilizations" existed throughout Africa, where "great kings" ruled "in might and wisdom over vast empires." After Egypt declined, magnificent empires arose in West Africa, in Ghana, Mali, Songhay—all marked by the brilliance and enlightenment of their administration and the high quality of their libraries and universities. Then Moorish invaders from the north plundered the black empires and sent West Africa into decline. European slave traders thereafter invented "fantastic tales of savagery about Africans" so that the slave trade would appear an act of Christian charity. Clarke concedes that slavery existed in West Africa before the Europeans arrived, but it was, he suggests, a humane and kindly servitude. The subsequent deterioration of Africa was caused by "the greed and imperialistic goals of the European nations."

Other Baseline Essays argue in a similar vein that Africa was the birthplace of science, mathematics, philosophy, medicine, and art, and that Europe stole its civilization from Africa and then engaged in "malicious misrepresentation of African society and people . . . to support the enormous profitability of slavery." "It was not done by accident," adds Leonard Jeffries. "It was done as part of a conspiracy to prevent us from having a unified experience." The coordinator of multicultural/multi-ethnic education in Portland even says that Napoleon personally shot off the nose of the Sphinx so that the Sphinx would not be recognized as African.

Like other excluded groups before them, black Americans invoke supposed past glories to compensate for real past and present injustices. Because their exclusion has been more tragic and terrible than that of white immigrants, their quest for self-affirmation is more intense and passionate. In seeking to impose Afrocentric curricula on public schools, for example, they go further than their white predecessors. And belated recognition by white America of the wrongs so viciously inflicted on black Americans has created the phenomenon of white guilt—not a bad thing in many respects, but still a vulnerability that invites cynical black exploitation and manipulation.

The black American predicament is another variation on the familiar theme of nationalism. No American scholar has written more fondly about the Arab quest for identity or has more sharply accused the West of imperialism and racism than the Palestinian-American Edward W. Said of Columbia. Yet Said sees in his beloved Arab Middle East the pathos of "an aggrieved and unfulfilled nationalism, beset with conspiracies." He warns against "the provincial and self-pitying posture that argues that a largely fictional and monolithic West disdains us. . . . There are many Wests, some antagonistic, some not." He warns too against "thinkers who want to start from scratch and zealously, not to say furiously, take things back to some pure, sacred origin. This has given all sorts of pathologies time and space enough to take hold." Serious black scholars see the black predicament with similar clarity.

History as a weapon is an abuse of history. The high purpose of history is not the presentation of self nor the vindication of identity but the recognition of complexity and the search for knowledge. "We need odes not to blood and mythology or uprooted, mourned or dead plants," writes Said, "but to living creatures and actual situations."

3

☆ ☆ ☆ ☆

The Battle of the Schools

There is nothing more natural than for black Americans, as wounded racial groups have done through history, to assert pride and claim identity and, because black wounds are so much deeper than white, to do so with tragic intensity. Nor is there anything more natural than for generous-hearted people, black and white, to go along with Afrocentrism out of a decent sympathy for the insulted and injured of American society and of a decent concern to bind up the wounds. Still, doctrinaire ethnicity in general and the dogmatic black version in

particular raise questions that deserve careful and dispassionate examination.

I

Cultural pluralism is a necessity in an ethnically diversified society. But the motives behind curriculum reform
sometimes go beyond the desire for a more honest representation of the past. "Multiculturalism" arises as a reaction against Anglo- or Eurocentrism; but at what point
does it mutate into an ethnocentrism of its own? The
very word, instead of referring as it should to all cultures,
has come to refer only to non-Western, nonwhite cultures. The president of the Modern Language Association even wonders why "we cannot be students of
Western culture and multiculturalism at the same time."

I am constrained to feel that the cult of ethnicity in
general and the Afrocentric campaign in particular do
not bode well either for American education or for the
future of the minorities. I would like to pose some of the
questions that worry me.

Little is harder to talk honestly about in America
these days than race. Too many sensitivities are involved,
too many opportunities for misunderstanding. I may perhaps be pardoned if I try to make clear where I come
from. Both by inheritance and by conviction I believe in
the pluralistic approach to the writing and teaching of
history. My father was his generation's great champion of
social history, of urban history, of immigration history.
He was an active member—in the end, the last white
member—of the executive council of the Association for

the Study of Negro Life and History and a staunch friend
of its director, the noted black historian Carter G. Woodson, and of such other black scholars as Charles Wesley,
W. M. Brewer, Rayford W. Logan, Alruthius Taylor, and
John Hope Franklin.

As for me, I was for a time a member of the executive council of the *Journal of Negro History.* I wrote in
that journal 30 years ago that black history is "essential if
we are to know in its majesty and terror the real history
of the United States." I believe in the importance of
teaching Americans the history of other cultures—East
Asia, Latin America, the Middle East, Africa, Polynesia.
I have been a lifelong advocate of civil rights.

Cultural pluralism is not the issue. Nor is the teaching of Afro-American or African history the issue; of
course these are legitimate subjects. Nor is multiculturalism, properly construed, the issue. The issue is the ethnocentric history that the New York task force, the
Portland Baseline essayists, and other Afrocentric ideologues propose for American children. The issue is the
teaching of *bad* history under whatever ethnic banner.
Can any historian justify the proposition that the five ethnic communities into which the New York state task force
wishes to divide the country had equal influence on the
development of the United States? Is it a function of
schools to teach ethnic and racial pride? When does obsession with differences begin to threaten the idea of an
overarching American nationality?

One argument for organizing a school curriculum
around Africa is that black Africa is the birthplace of science, philosophy, religion, medicine, technology, of the
great achievements that have been wrongly ascribed to

Western civilization. But is this in fact true? Many historians and anthropologists regard Mesopotamia as the cradle of civilization; for a recent discussion, see Charles Keith Maisels' *The Emergence of Civilization.* If there were as many Iraqi-Americans as there are black Americans, we would no doubt have a campaign for an Iraqocentric curriculum. But there aren't enough Iraqi-Americans, and, with Sadam Hussein, they have troubles of their own.

The Afrocentrist case rests largely on the proposition that ancient Egypt was essentially a black African country. I am far from being an expert on Egyptian history, but neither, one must add, are the educators and psychologists who push Afrocentrism. A book they often cite is Martin Bernal's *Black Athena,* a vigorous effort by a Cornell professor to document Egyptian influence on ancient Greece. In fact Bernal makes no very strong claims about Egyptian pigmentation; but, citing Herodotus, he does argue that several Egyptian dynasties "were made up of pharaohs whom one can usefully call black."

Frank M. Snowden Jr., the distinguished black classicist at Howard University and author of *Blacks in Antiquity,* is most doubtful about painting ancient Egypt black. Bernal's assumption that Herodotus meant black in the twentieth-century sense is contradicted, Snowden demonstrates, "by Herodotus himself and the copious evidence of other classical authors." Frank J. Yurco, an Egyptologist at Chicago's Field Museum of Natural History, after examining the evidence derivable from mummies, paintings, statues, and relies, concludes in the *Biblical Archaeological Review* that ancient Egyptians, like their modern descendants, varied in color from the light Mediterranean type to the darker brown of upper Egypt to the still darker shade of the Nubians around Aswan. He adds that ancient Egyptians would have found the question meaningless and wonders at our presumption in assigning "our primitive racial labels" to so impressive a culture.

Yurco's verdict on John Henrik Clarke's Baseline Essay exposition of the Afrocentric case is comprehensive—"a mélange of misinformation, inconsistence [*sic*], outright fallacious information, half-truths, and outdated information . . . virtually valueless as scholarship . . . reads more like a medieval chronicle in parts than like a current survey of history."

The classical scholar Mary Lefkowitz in her book *Not Out of Africa* and the historians assembled in the book she edited with G. M. Rogers, *Black Athena Revisited,* subject Afrocentric historical fantasies to learned demolition. "This book," the Ghanian scholar K. Anthony Appiah writes of *Not Out of Africa,* "is the best word so far in the debate about Egypt's influence on classical Greek philosophy." It goes far to settling the debate.

II

After Egypt, Afrocentrists teach children about the glorious West African emperors, the vast lands they ruled, the civilization they achieved; not, however, about the tyrannous authority they exercised, the ferocity of their wars, the tribal massacres, the squalid lot of the common people, the captives sold into slavery, the complicity with the Atlantic slave trade, the persistence of slavery in Africa after it was abolished in the West.

As for tribalism, the word *tribe* hardly occurs in the Afrocentric lexicon; but who can hope to understand African history without understanding the practices, loyalties, rituals, blood-feuds of tribalism? Black historians of an earlier generation, like Carter Woodson, wrote of the "orgies of war and sacrifice of human beings" in West African societies. That note is not struck in the Afrocentric curriculum.

One can go on indefinitely citing dubious claims Afrocentrist ideologues represent as facts—that Pythagoras and Aristotle, for example, stole their mathematics and philosophy from black scholars in Egypt. But there is no reliable evidence that either Pythagoras or Aristotle ever visited Egypt. In the case of Pythagoras, writes Professor L. Pearce Williams, the Cornell historian of science, the Babylonians and Egyptians certainly were acquainted with the Pythagorean relationship, but the Pythagorean theorems, the proof of the relationship, were Hellenic. In the case of Aristotle, the notion that Alexander the Great pillaged the Library of Alexandria on his old tutor's behalf falls before the facts that there was no Alexandria to pillage until Alexander founded the city and that the library was not established until half a century after Alexander and Aristotle died. In any case, ideas can hardly be "stolen"—totally removed from the original owner—like jewels. As Diane Ravitch sensibly asks, how in the world does one "lose knowledge by sharing it"?

The Baseline Essay on science and technology contains biographies of black American scientists, among them Charles R. Drew, who first developed the process for the preservation of blood plasma. In 1950 Drew, grievously injured in an automobile accident in North Carolina, lost quantities of blood. "*Not one* of several nearby white hospitals," according to the Baseline Essay, "would provide the blood transfusions he so desparately [*sic*] needed, and on the way to a hospital that treated Black people, he died." It is a hell of a story—the inventor of blood-plasma storage dead because racist whites denied him his own invention. Only it is not true. As Spencie Love conclusively shows in her biography *One Blood: The Death and Resurrection of Charles R. Drew,* "Drew had been promptly taken to one hospital and appropriately treated there by three white surgeons. He died in the emergency room." (She also points out why the legend spread: even if Dr. Drew was not denied emergency care, too, many other black Americans were.)

Is it really a good idea to teach minority children myths—at least to teach myths as facts? A reporter for the *Oregonian* describes what is going on these days in Portland classrooms: "[black students] have learned, for example, that Africans visited the Americas long before Columbus did and that Cleopatra was black." Is Afrocentric chauvinism any different from the Irish-American myth-making satirized by John V. Kelleher? Does not this uncritical glorification carry us back to Plato's "noble lies"?

III

The deeper reason for the Afrocentric campaign lies in the theory that the purpose of history in the schools is essentially therapeutic: to build a sense of self-worth among minority children. Eurocentrism, by denying nonwhite children any past in which they can take pride, is held to be the cause of poor academic performance. Race consciousness and group pride are supposed to strengthen a sense of identity and self-respect among nonwhite students.

Everyone is distressed over the state of American education, especially in our cities. Everyone is concerned with the search for remedies, especially remedies that will not require money and increase taxes. Curriculum revision costs little; it appeases militant nonwhite minorities; it relieves guilt feelings among the white majority. It might even work. Or will it? Does Afrocentrism have much possibility of working even in its own terms?

Will black children really do better in school if they are taught that everything good in the world came out of Africa? This proposition assumes a live connection between black America and Africa, and especially Egypt as Afrocentrism's prime exhibit. But any relationship between Egyptians, whatever color they may have been, and black Americans is exceedingly tenuous.

Black Americans do not trace their roots to Egypt. The great majority of their ancestors came from West Africa, especially the Guinea coast. They were from a variety of tribes and spoke a variety of languages; Professor

Ali Mazrui tells us that Africa contains some 850 distinct ethnic and linguistic groups. Any homogeneity among slaves derived not from the African tribe but from the American plantation.

But what about Afrocentricity and the proposition that the black mind works in a genetically different way? May there not be abiding psychological and biological ties to Africa? The "unique status" of black psychology, claims the black psychologist Wade Nobles, derives from "basic African philosophy which dictates the values, cus-. toms, attitudes, and behavior of Africans in Africa and the New World." This line of thought has obvious affinities with Léopold Senghor's concept of Negritude, which in its original formulation saw blacks everywhere as genetically endowed with distinctive human values, psychological makeup, and cultural style. "Emotion is Negro," said Senghor, "as reason is Hellenic."

But unless one is to yield to biological determinism and accept that the possession of black skin creates a unique black mentality and character, it is hard to see what living connection exists between American blacks today and their heterogeneous West African ancestors three centuries ago. And biological determinism—the theory that race determines mentality—is of course just another word for racism. Biological determinism is exactly the theory apologists for slavery used in the American South before the Civil War. It is bizarre to hear blacks invoking the same theory today.

Until very recent times, few black Americans have regarded the African connection as a major theme in their lives. David Walker, in his 1829 *Appeal . . . to the Colored Citizens of the World,* said of America, "This land which we have watered with our *tears* and our *blood* is now our mother country." "No one idea has given rise to more oppression and persecution toward the colored people of this country," wrote the great Frederick Douglass, "than that which makes Africa, not America, their home. It is that wolfish idea that elbows us off the side walk, and denies us the rights of citizenship." When the freedmen after emancipation chose last names, they took not African names but the names of American heroes— Washington, Jefferson, Jackson, Clay, Lincoln. "Centuries of residence, centuries of toil, centuries of suffering have made us Americans," a black high-school principal in Ohio said in 1874. "In language, in civilization, in fears, and in hopes we are Americans."

"Neither my father nor my father's father ever saw Africa," recalled W. E. B. Du Bois, "or knew its meaning or cared overmuch for it." His own black associates in the National Association for the Advancement of Colored People, Du Bois recalled, had a "fierce repugnance toward anything African. . . . They felt themselves Americans, not Africans. They resented and feared any coupling with Africa." Though Du Bois himself spent his last years in West Africa, he had earlier dismissed the African connection: "Once for all, let us realize that we are Americans, that we were brought here with the earliest settlers and that the very sort of civilization from which we came made the complete absorption of Western modes and customs imperative if we were to survive at all; in brief, *there is nothing so indigenous, so completely 'made in America' as we.*"

From time to time, black leaders, notably Martin

Delany in the mid-nineteenth century and Marcus Garvey in the 1920s, excited passing interest in Africa. But Delany's campaign was derailed by the Civil War, and Garvey was a Jamaican who developed his back-to-Africa vision in England; his American influence was short-lived. Mussolini's attack on Ethiopia in 1935 set off another spasm of interest, again short-lived.

I recall the 1956 presidential campaign. Adlai Stevenson, for whom I was working, had a weak record on civil rights in America but a strong record on nationalism in Africa. I suggested to a group of sympathetic black leaders that maybe if Stevenson talked to black audiences about Africa for the Africans, he could make up for his deficiencies on civil rights. My friends laughed and said that American blacks couldn't care less about Africa.

"Nor can the American Negro," wrote Abram L. Harris, the radical black economist, "be considered in any logical way African." The black educator Horace Mann Bond spoke in 1959 of "the American Negro's traditional aversion to Africa and things African." In 1964 the sociologist Milton Gordon wrote about black Americans, "Their sense of identification with ancestral African national cultures is virtually nonexistent." "The Negro is an American," Martin Luther King Jr., told Robert Penn Warren. "We know nothing of Africa."

Countee Cullen's poem sums it up:

> What is Africa to me:
> Copper sun or scarlet sea,
> Jungle star or jungle track,

Strong bronzed men, or regal black
Women from whose loins I sprang
When the birds of Eden sang?

*One three centuries removed
From the scenes his fathers loved,
Spicy grove, cinnamon tree,
What is Africa to me?*

IV

Obviously attitudes toward Africa have changed markedly in the last 25 years. But American Afrocentrism is really a case of what the English historian Eric Hobsbawm calls "the invention of tradition." Alex Haley's compelling *Roots* helped create an audience for the tradition—though, as Ishmael Reed later observed, if Haley had traced his father's rather than his mother's bloodline, "he would have traveled 12 generations back to, not Gambia, but *Ireland.*"

The great stimulus was less the civil rights revolution, which had rushed along without benefit of Afrocentrism, than it was the pride generated by the appearance of independent African states—for many American blacks a proof of racial virility, as the establishment of Israel was for many American Jews. The analogy is incomplete. Where Jewish-Americans can (or could until recently) look with pride on the achievements of Israel, African-Americans, hard put to find much to admire in contemporary Liberia or Uganda or Ghana, must instead seek moments of glory in the dim past.

The glorification of the African past was accompanied by a campaign to replace Anglo "slave" names with African names, to wear African costumes, to replicate African rituals. LeRoi Jones, who had said in 1962 that "history for the Negro, before America, must remain an emotional abstraction," now saw Africa more concretely and changed his name to Amiri Baraka. Arthur Smith became Molefi Kete Asante and called on others to embrace African names: "only such a name reflects our consciousness."

At Asa Hilliard's conference "Infusion of African and African-American Content in the School Curriculum," John Henrik Clarke was honored by the Ashanti Enstoolment ceremony: first, the blowing of a shell-horn and the beating of drums, then the lowering of Clarke three times onto the seat of respect. "Five bare-chested men in sashes, with gold bangles around their heads, paraded in," reports Andrew Sullivan in *The New Republic,* "carrying a vast yellow parasol topped by a small ivory elephant."

In another session Abena Walker said that Afrocentric education in the District of Columbia would lean heavily on ritual, music, and mantras; children would "learn through rhythm and rapping." Wade Nobles, dressed in a lilac-blue robe, carried to the podium a fetish to ward off evil and observed the African custom of seeking the permission of elders before beginning to speak. "When we adopt other people's theories," he proceeded to say, "we are like Frankenstein [he meant Frankenstein's monster] doing other people's wills. It's like someone drinking some good stuff, vomiting it, and then we have to catch the vomit and drink it ourselves. . . . Don't become the vomit-drinkers!"

Surely there is something a little sad about all this—quite beyond the vulgar outburst that dismisses the Western intellectual heritage as vomit. There is little evidence, however, that such invention of tradition is much more than the pastime of a few angry, ambitious, and perhaps despairing zealots and hustlers. Their impact is greater on the guilt of whites than on the common sense of the black community.

The Africanization of black Americans has not got very far. Perhaps this is because, as the black historian Nathan Huggins has written, "An Afro-American and the grandson of a Polish immigrant will be able to take more for granted between themselves than the former could with a Nigerian or the latter with a Warsaw worker." As even Asante concedes, when black Americans visit Africa, Africans perceive them as plain Americans and hardly as African at all.

Anyone who knows anything about Africa, the black columnist William Raspberry of *The Washington Post* has written, knows that there is no single "African" culture from which black Americans are descended. "While some Africans were establishing a university at Timbuktu, others were engaged in slavery or tribal warfare or cannibalism. Some Africans were monotheists, while others were animists. As with their European counterparts, some were promoting brilliant philosophies, while others were savages." As for the Afrocentric curriculum, Raspberry adds, it is a "questionable assumption that black children, with only the vaguest notions of their African ancestry, can be inculcated with African culture more easily than the American culture to which they are daily exposed."

Black Peace Corps volunteers in Africa, as David Riesman, the sociologist and Peace Corps adviser, observed, returned from their ancestral to their "real" homes with new awareness of their "fundamental Americanness." In the end, they found themselves children of—contributors to, casualties of—American culture, not of African culture.

V

Even if black America had a spontaneous and authentic relationship with Africa, would learning about Africa improve the self-esteem of black children?

The New York curricular-revision task force claims that the monocultural Eurocentric bias has "a terribly damaging effect on the psyche of young people of African, Asian, Latino, and Native American descent." The idea that Europe has produced one homogeneous culture seems rather weird. What is so "monocultural" about the wild mix of people from Reykjavík to Athens and from Lisbon to Omsk? Can Henry Adams and the person he once described as "a furtive Yacoob or Ysaac still reeking of the Ghetto, snarling a weird Yiddish to the officers of the customs" be usefully regarded as products of a single culture? Churchill and Hitler, St. Francis and Machiavelli, Pericles and Dracula—monocultural?

In any event, the task-force report vouchsafes no proof for the assertion that a Eurocentric bias wrecks the psyches of minority children. So far as I can find out, there is no empirical study showing that high self-esteem leads to superior academic performance. Indeed, high self-esteem often goes along with low performance. Experts on the famed California Task Force on Self-Esteem concluded that "associations between self-esteem and its expected consequences are mixed, insignificant, or absent."

The theory is that immersion in the history of one's own group will overcome feelings of racial inferiority both by instilling pride in past ethnic accomplishments and by providing ethnic role models to inspire future performance. Telling black children how marvelous old Africa was will make them work harder and do better. But does study of the glory that was Greece and the grandeur that was Rome improve the academic record of Greek-American and Italian-American children? Not so that anyone has noticed. Why is it likely to help black children, who are removed from their geographical origins not by 50 years but by 300?

Nor does the absence of historical role models seem to have handicapped two other groups in American society—Jewish-Americans and Asian-Americans. There are no Semitocentric or Asiacentric public-school curricula glorifying the civilization of their ancestors. Yet Jewish-Americans and even more particularly Asian-Americans—3 percent of the population, 30 percent of the students at Berkeley—have academic success out of proportion to their numbers in the population.

After the original and immoderate task force report in New York, the Commissioner of Education appointed a new committee that, in due course, produced a report a good deal more moderate in its argument but still somewhat divisive in its implications. Students, the report recommended, should be "continually" encouraged to ask themselves what their cultural heritage is, why they should be proud of it, "why should I develop an understanding of and respect for my own culture(s), language(s), religion, and national origin(s)."

But would it not be more appropriate for students to be "continually" encouraged to understand the American culture in which they are growing up and to prepare for an active role in shaping that culture? "If I am a newcomer to your country," says the Mexican-American writer Richard Rodriguez, "why teach me about my ancestors? I need to know about 17th century Puritans in order to make sense of the rebellion I notice everywhere in the American city. Teach me about mad British kings so I will understand the American penchant for iconoclasm. Then teach me about cowboys and Indians; I should know that tragedies created the country that will create me." Should public education strengthen and perpetuate separate ethnic and racial subcultures? or should it not seek to make our young boys and girls contributors to a common American culture?

Let me make one exception to the general proposition—the case of the American Indians. For they are the inheritors and guardians of unique cultures of which they are sole possessors. If Italian-Americans, for example, lose connection with their ancestral culture, that does not mean the extinction of Italian culture. After all, Italy will still be there. But if Indians lose connection with their cultures, those cultures disappear forever, and humankind is thereby diminished. There was a melancholy headline on the obituary page of the *New York Times* in 1996: "Red Thunder Cloud, 86, Dies and the Catawba Tongue With Him." So in the special case of the American Indian, the protection of separate communities would seem justified.

But in general one senses a certain inauthenticity in saddling public schools with the mission of convincing children of the beauties of their particular ethnic origins. Ethnic subcultures, if they had genuine vitality, would be sufficiently instilled in children by family, church, and community. It is surely not the office of the public school to promote artificial ethnic chauvinism.

VI

Why does anyone suppose that pride and inspiration are available only from people of the same ethnicity? Can only relatives be role models? Plainly this is not the case. At the age of 12, Frederick Douglass encountered a book entitled *The Columbian Orator* containing speeches by Burke, Sheridan, Pitt, and Fox. "Every opportunity I got," Douglass later said, "I used to read this book." The orations "gave tongue to interesting thoughts of my own soul, which had frequently flashed through my mind, and died away for want of utterance. . . . What I got from Sheridan was a bold denunciation of slavery and a powerful vindication of human rights. The reading of these documents enabled me to utter my thoughts." Douglass did not find the fact that the orators were white an insuperable obstacle.

Nor did W. E. B. Du Bois shrink from contact with

the Eurocentric tradition. "I sit with Shakespeare and he winces not. Across the color line I move arm in arm with Balzac and Dumas, where smiling men and welcoming women glide in gilded halls. . . . I summon Aristotle and Aurelius and what soul I will, and they come all graciously with no scorn nor condescension. So, wed with Truth, I dwell above the veil."

Or hear Ralph Ellison: "In Macon County, Alabama, I read Marx, Freud, T. S. Eliot, Pound, Gertrude Stein, and Hemingway. Books which seldom, if ever, mentioned Negroes were to release me from whatever 'segregated' idea I might have had of my human possibilities." He was freed, Ellison continued, not by the example of Richard Wright and other black writers but by artists who offered a broader sense of life and possibility. "It requires real poverty of the imagination to think that this can come to a Negro only through the example of other Negroes." As he added many years later, when the black writer Charles Johnson won the National Book Award for *Middle Passage,* "You don't write out of your skin, for God's sake, you write out of your imagination."

When Sterling Brown, Arthur P. Davis, and Ulysses Lee brought out their influential anthology of black writing, *The Negro Caravan,* in 1941, they disclaimed the notion that black writing falls "into a unique cultural pattern. . . . Many contemporary Negro writers are closer to O. Henry, Carl Sandburg, Edgar Lee Masters, Edna St. Vincent Millay, Waldo Frank, Ernest Hemingway, and John Steinbeck than to each other. The bonds of literary tradition seem to be stronger than race."

Martin Luther King Jr., did pretty well with Thoreau, Gandhi, and Reinhold Niebuhr as models—

and remember, after all, for whom King (and his father) were named. The record hardly shows that "Eurocentric" education had such a terribly damaging effect on the psyche of great black Americans. Why deny it to black children today? Why not dwell with Du Bois above the veil? Is Lincoln to be a hero only for those of English ancestry? Jackson only for Scotch-Irish? Douglass only for blacks? Great artists, thinkers, leaders are the possession not just of their own racial clan but of all humanity.

As for self-esteem, is this really the product of ethnic role models and fantasies of a glorious past? or does it not result from the belief in oneself that springs from achievement, from personal rather than from racial pride? Cohesive Asian-American and Jewish-American families instill in their children a sense of self-respect and a determination to work hard. For historical reasons, black families are often less cohesive, and in consequence many black kids often move into a mistrustful world with low self-worth and little self-confidence. Hearing about Africa won't change that.

VII

The use of history as therapy means the corruption of history as history. All major races, cultures, nations have committed crimes, atrocities, horrors at one time or another. Every civilization has skeletons in its closet. Honest history calls for the unexpurgated record. How much would a full account of African despotism, massacre, and slavery increase the self-esteem of black students? Yet what kind of history do you have if you leave out all the bad things?

Even if history is sanitized in order to make people feel good, there is no evidence that feel-good history promotes ethnic self-esteem and equips students to grapple with their lives. Afrocentric education, on the contrary, will make black children, as William Raspberry has written, "less competent in the culture in which they have to compete." After all, what good will it do young black Americans to take African names, wear African costumes, and replicate African rituals, to learn by music and mantras, rhythm and rapping, to reject standard English, to hear that because their minds work differently a first-class education is not for them? Will such training help them to understand democracy better? Help them to fit better into American life? "General Powell did not reach his present post," Jacques Barzun reminds us, "by believing that Black English was sufficient for the career he wanted to pursue."

Indeed, it is hard to imagine any form of education more likely than Afrocentrism to have a "terribly damaging effect on the psyche." The best way to keep a people down is to deny them the means of improvement and achievement and cut them off from the opportunities of the national life. If some Kleagle of the Ku Klux Klan wanted to devise an educational curriculum for the specific purpose of handicapping and disabling black Americans, he would not be likely to come up with anything more diabolically effective than Afrocentrism.

Moreover, will it increase their self-esteem when black children grow up and learn that many of the things the Afrocentrists taught them are not true? Black scholars have tried for years to rescue black history from chauvinistic hyperbole. A. A. Schomburg, the noted archivist of black history, expressed his scorn long ago for those who "glibly tried to prove that half of the world's geniuses have been Negroes and to trace the pedigree of nineteenth-century Americans from the Queen of Sheba."

The black sociologist Orlando Patterson writes with similar scorn of black educators who "head for the civilizational big-time: to Carthage and Egypt and Nubia and the rest of the 'great' civilizations of ancient North Africa. . . . The role of the Black historian is to get the Black man back into the wonderful 'birth of civilization' story, to prove that white history has been a big lie, that the Black man . . . was right there in all the major events of 'world history.' " Patterson calls it the three P's approach: black history as princes, pyramids, and pageantry.

The dean of black historians in America today is John Hope Franklin. "While a black scholar," Franklin writes, "has a clear responsibility to join in improving the society in which he lives, he must understand the difference between hard-hitting advocacy on the one hand and the highest standards of scholarship on the other." Serious black scholars like Henry Louis Gates Jr., and the group he has assembled in the department of Afro-American studies at Harvard, reject Afrocentricity.

Afrocentrists are advocates not of multiculturalism but of black ethnocentrism. Nor do they make much effort to disguise political motives. Asa Hilliard deals with scholarly critics not by responding to their criticisms but by calling any attack on the Afrocentric curriculum "an attack on the study of African people generally." Defending the New York task-force report, one of its authors called the proposed curricular revision "a powerful tool of cultural and political empowerment. I see a clear relationship in the effort to keep us weak and the recognition that we [the non-whites] will be the majority in the 21st century." It is notable how few respected black scholars attended Hilliard's 1990 convention, "The Infusion of African and African American Content in the School Curriculum."

VIII

"Once ethnic pride and self-esteem become the criterion for teaching history," Diane Ravitch points out, "certain things cannot be taught." Skeletons must stay in the closet lest outing displease descendants.

No history curriculum in the country is more carefully wrought and better balanced in its cultural pluralism than California's. But hearings before the State Board of Education show what happens when ethnicity is unleashed at the expense of scholarship. At issue were textbooks responsive to the new curriculum. Polish-Americans demanded that any reference to Hitler's holocaust be matched by tales of equivalent genocide suffered by Polish Christians. Armenian-Americans sought coverage of Turkish massacres; Turkish-Americans objected. Though serious black historians testified that the treatment of black history was examplary, Afrocentrists said the schoolbooks would lead to

"textbook genocide." Moslems complained that an illus-
tration of an Islamic warrior with a raised scimitar stereo-
typed Moslems as "terrorists."

"One group after another," Ravitch recalls, "insisted
that its forebears had suffered more than anyone else in
history." American Indians, Hispanics, Chinese-
Americans, homosexuals, born-again Christian fundamentalists, atheists—all protested that the schoolbooks
had not gone far enough in celebrating their particular
cultures or viewpoints. "The single theme that persistently ran through the hearings," Ravitch writes, "was
that the critics did not want anything taught if it offended
members of their group; whatever was taught, many
claimed, must have a positive effect on the self-esteem or
pride of their group. . . . The only villains in the history-
for-self-esteem movement . . . are white males, who thus
far have no spokesmen."

In New York the curriculum guide for 11th-grade
American history tells students that there were three
"foundations" for the Constitution: the European Enlightenment, the "Haudenosaunee political system," and
the antecedent colonial experience. Only the Haudenosaunee political system receives explanatory sub-
headings: "a. Influence upon colonial leadership and
European intellectuals (Locke, Montesquieu, Voltaire,
Rousseau); b. Impact on Albany Plan of Union, Articles
of Confederation, and U. S. Constitution."

How many experts on the American Constitution
would endorse this stirring tribute to the "Haudenosaunee political system"? How many have heard of
that system? Whatever influence the Iroquois confederation may have had on the framers of the Constitution

was marginal; on European intellectuals it was marginal to the point of invisibility. No other state curriculum offers this analysis of the making of the Constitution. But then no other state has so effective an Iroquois lobby.

Perhaps inspired by the success of the Iroquois lobby, an Irish-American lobby in 1996 pushed a bill through the New York legislature requiring instruction in human rights "with particular attention to . . . genocide, slavery, the Holocaust, and the mass starvation in Ireland from 1845 to 1850"—a tragedy the bill attributed to British policy. How many other ethnic lobbies will seek to mold public school instruction to their own purposes?

The debate over the New York history curriculum produced thoughtful reactions from the state's history teachers. History, one wrote, "should not be a vehicle for pleasing or appeasing any social group, nor should teachers act as public-relations counselors for a cause. Writing history requires a critical analysis of a topic and not a laudatory exposition of its exploits." The Department of History at the State University of New York College at Brockport summed the question up in a circular letter to departments of history throughout the state: "We insist that the curriculum not be used as an instrument that is primarily designed to redress past injustices, however real. It is, rather, a tool with which to pursue the truths about our common past."

President Franklyn Jenifer of Howard University, while saying that "historical black institutions" like his own have a responsibility to teach young people about their particular history and culture, added, "One has to be very careful when one is talking about public schools. . . . Public schools by their definition are schools that are open to all people, and should be cognizant of the needs of all of the people. . . . There should be no creation of nonexistent history."

When every ethnic and religious group claims a right to approve or veto anything that is taught in public schools, cultural pluralism becomes ethnocentrism. An evident casualty is the old idea that whatever our ethnic base, we are all Americans together.

Feel-good history, moreover, is a betrayal of a noble profession. "What I hate," Gore Vidal has well said, "is good citizenship history. That has wrecked every history book. Now we're getting, 'The Hispanics are warm and joyous and have brought such wonder into our lives,' you know, and before them the Jews, and before them the blacks. And the women. I mean, cut it out!"

Let us by all means teach black history, African history, women's history, Hispanic history, Asian history. But let us teach them as history, not as filiopietistic commemoration. The purpose of history is to promote not group self-esteem, but understanding of the world and the past, dispassionate analysis, judgment, and perspective, respect for divergent cultures and traditions, and unflinching protection for those unifying ideas of tolerance, democracy, and human rights that make free historical inquiry possible.

4

☆ ☆ ☆ ☆

The Decomposition
of America

L ow self-esteem is too deep a malady to be cured by
hearing nice things about one's own ethnic past. History is not likely to succeed where psychiatry fails. Afrocentrism in particular is an escape from the hard and
expensive challenges of our society—the need for safer
schools, better teachers, better teaching materials,
greater investment in education; the need for stable families that can nourish self-discipline and aspiration; the
need for jobs and income that can nourish stable families;
the need to stop the ravages of drugs and crime; the need

to overcome the racism still lurking in the interstices of American society. "The need," William Raspberry observes of his own people, "is not to reach back for some culture we never knew but to lay full claim to the culture in which we exist."

I

The ethnicity rage in general and Afrocentricity in particular not only divert attention from the real needs but exacerbate the problems. The recent apotheosis of ethnicity, black, brown, red, yellow, white, has revived the dismal prospect that in melting-pot days Americans thought the republic was moving safely beyond—that is, a society fragmented into separate ethnic communities. The cult of ethnicity exaggerates differences, intensifies resentments and antagonisms, drives ever deeper the awful wedges between races and nationalities. The endgame is self-pity and self-ghettoization.

Now there is a reasonable argument in the black case for a measure of regrouping and self-reliance as part of the preparation for entry into an integrated society on an equal basis. Integration on any other basis, it is contended, would mean total capitulation to white standards. Affirmation of racial and cultural pride is thus essential to true integration. One can see this as a psychological point, but as a cultural point?

For generations blacks have grown up in an American culture, on which they have had significant influence and to which they have made significant contributions. Self-Africanization after 300 years in America is playacting. Afrocentricity as expounded by ethnic ideologues implies Europhobia, separatism, emotions of alienation, victimization, paranoia. Most curious and unexpected of all is a black demand for the return of black-white segregation.

"To separate [black children] from others of similar age and qualifications solely because of their race," Chief Justice Warren wrote in the school-integration case, "generates a feeling of inferiority as to their status in the community that may affect their hearts and minds in a way unlikely ever to be undone." In 40 years doctrine has come full circle. Now integration is held to bring feelings of inferiority, and segregation to bring the cure.

This revival of separatism will begin, if the black educator Felix Boateng has his way, in the earliest grades. "The use of standard English as the only language of instruction," Boateng argues, "aggravates the process of deculturalization." A "culturally relevant curriculum" for minority children would recognize "the home and community dialect they bring to school." (Not all black educators, it should be said, share this desire to handicap black children from infancy. "One fact is clear," notes Janice Hale-Benson of Cleveland State University. "Speaking standard English is a skill needed by Black children for upward mobility in American society and it should be taught in early childhood.")

If any educational institution should bring people together as individuals in friendly and civil association, it should be the university. But the fragmentation of campuses in recent years into a multitude of ethnic organizations is spectacular—and disconcerting.

One finds black dormitories, black student unions,

black fraternities and sororities, black business and law societies, black homosexual and lesbian groups, black tables in dining halls. The University of Pennsylvania gives blacks—6 percent of the enrollment—their own yearbook. Campuses today, according to one University of Pennsylvania professor, have "the cultural diversity of Beirut. There are separate armed camps. The black kids don't mix with the white kids. The Asians are off by themselves. Oppression is the great status symbol." In 1994 Brown University suspended the spread of "theme" houses. "We don't want to have a Balkanization of the campus," said the executive vice president.

Oberlin was for a century and a half the model of a racially integrated college. "Increasingly," Jacob Weisberg, an editor at *The New Republic*, reports, "Oberlin students think, act, study, and live apart." Asians live in Asia House, Jews in "J" House, Latinos in Spanish House, blacks in African-Heritage House, foreign students in Third World House. Even the Lesbian, Gay, and Bisexual Union has broken up into racial and gender factions. "The result is separate worlds."

Huddling is an understandable reaction for any minority group faced with new and scary challenges. But institutionalized separatism only crystallizes racial differences and magnifies racial tensions. "Certain activities are labeled white and black," says a black student at Central Michigan University. "If you don't just participate in black activities, you are shunned." A recent study by the black anthropologist Signithia Fordham of Rutgers concludes that a big reason for black underachievement is the fear that academic success will be taken as a sellout to the white world. "What appears to have emerged in some segments of the black community," Fordham says, "is a kind of cultural orientation which defines academic learning in school as 'acting white.' "

Militants further argue that because only blacks can comprehend the black experience, only blacks should teach black history and literature, as, in the view of some feminists, only women should teach women's history and literature. "True diversity," according to the faculty's Budget Committee at the University of California at Berkeley, requires that courses match the ethnic and gender identities of the professors.

The doctrine that *only* blacks can teach and write black history leads inexorably to the doctrine that blacks can teach and write *only* black history as well as to inescapable corollaries: Chinese must be restricted to Chinese history, women to women's history, and so on. Henry Louis Gates criticizes "ghettoized programs where students and members of the faculty sit around and argue about whether a white person can think a black thought." As for the notion that there is a "mystique" about black studies that requires a person to have black skin in order to pursue them—that, John Hope Franklin observes succinctly, is "voodoo."

The voodoo principle is extended from scholarship to the arts. A current demand in the theater is that actors must have the same ethnicity as the parts they assume. Thus Actors' Equity Association tried to stop Jonathan Pryce from playing in New York the role he created in London in *Miss Saigon,* announcing piously that it could not condone "the casting of a Caucasian actor in the role of a Eurasian." Shirley MacLaine, acting a Jewish woman in the movie *Used People,* reports that her friend Bella

Abzug "was furious with me. . . . She thought a Jew should play the part."

The consanguinity principle is extended to directors. Thus Norman Jewison was vetoed as the director of *Malcolm X* because he was the wrong color. Spike Lee, who was the right color, got the job and then carried the rule to the extent of proclaiming a preference for black interviewers. The fine black playwright August Wilson insists on a black director for the film of his play *Fences*. "We have a different way of responding to the world," he said. "We have different ideas about religion, different manners of social intercourse. We have different ideas about style, about language. We have different esthetics. . . . The job requires someone who shares the specifics of the culture of black Americans. . . . Let's make a rule. Blacks don't direct Italian films. Italians don't direct Jewish films. Jews don't direct black American films."

By the Wilson rule, only Norwegians would be permitted to direct Ibsen, only Danes to play Hamlet. What a terrible rule that would be! As Jonathan Pryce observed during the *Miss Saigon* controversy, if the consanguinity principle should prevail, "I'd be stuck playing Welshmen for the rest of my life." Even self-righteous Equity did not apply that principle to the black actors Morgan Freeman and Denzel Washington when, at the height of the *Miss Saigon* brouhaha, they were acting Shakespeare (and not Othello) in New York. The *Wall Street Journal* suggested acidly that, if the principle was to control, not just whites but more especially the disabled ought to demonstrate against the casting of fully-abled Denzel

Washington as Richard III; after all, Richard III was a hunchback.

One sympathizes with the resentment of Chinese-American actors watching Swedes (as, for example, Warner Oland and Nils Asther in the old days) playing Chinese roles, and one rejoices at the breakthrough of nonwhite actors these days into stage and film. Yet is there not something basically hostile to the actor's art in the consanguinity principle? After all, what is acting but an exercise in dissimulation?

The challenge to actors is to create characters on the stage; and these characters may be very different from what the actors are in real life. That indeed is the actor's triumph. The racialist restriction nullifies the very essence of the actor's art. It equally nullifies the talent of directors. The idea that only Swedes can direct Strindberg, only Russians Chekhov, only Irish Sheridan or Shaw, only Englishmen Shakespeare is self-evidently ridiculous—and, if carried out, would hopelessly impoverish the art of the theater. The consanguinity principle is an exclusionary rule that penalizes the very minorities it claims to benefit.

The distinguished black social psychologist Kenneth B. Clark, whose findings influenced the Supreme Court's decision in the school-integration case, rejects the argument that blacks and whites must be separated "because they represent different cultures and that cultures, like oil and water, cannot mix." This, Clark says, is what white segregationists have argued for generations. He adds, "There is absolutely no evidence to support the contention that the inherent damage to human beings of primitive exclusion on the basis of race is any less damaging when demanded or enforced by the previous victims than when imposed by the dominant group."

II

The separatist impulse is by no means confined to the black community. Another salient expression is the bilingualism movement, ostensibly conducted in the interests of all non-English speakers but particularly a Hispanic-American project.

Bilingualism is hardly a new issue in American history. Seven years after the adoption of the Constitution, a proposal to print 3,000 sets of federal laws in German as well as English was narrowly defeated in the House of Representatives. (This incident gave rise to the myth, later cherished by Nazi propagandists like Colin Ross, that German had nearly displaced English as America's official language.) In the nineteenth century, newly arrived immigrants stayed for a season with their old language, used it in their homes, churches, newspapers, and not seldom in bilingual public schools, until acculturation reduced and the First World War discouraged the use of languages other than English.

In recent years the combination of the ethnicity cult with a flood of immigration from Spanish-speaking countries has given bilingualism new impetus. The presumed purpose is transitional: to move non-English-speaking children as quickly as possible from bilingual into all-English classes. The Bilingual Education Act of 1968 supplies guidelines and funding; the 1974 Supreme

Court decision in *Lau v. Nichols* (a Chinese-speaking case) requires school districts to provide special programs for children who do not know English.

Alas, bilingualism has not worked out as planned: rather the contrary. The bilingual campaign has created both an educational lobby with a vested interest in perpetuating a bilingual empire and a political lobby with a vested interest in retaining a Hispanic constituency. As a result, bilingual education in its current version does more to maintain Spanish than to teach English. Yet polls repeatedly show that Latino parents want their children taught in English. Many protest the retention of children with Hispanic names in Spanish-language classes. Like Afrocentricity and the ethnicity cult, bilingualism is not a popular but an elitist concern—"romantic ethnicity," Myrdal called it; political ethnicity too.

Institutionalized bilingualism shuts doors. It nourishes self-ghettoization, and ghettoization nourishes racial antagonism. Bilingualism "encourages concentrations of Hispanics to stay together and not be integrated," says Alfredo Mathew Jr., a Hispanic civic leader, and it may well foster "a type of apartheid that will generate animosities with others, such as Blacks, in the competition for scarce resources, and further alienate the Hispanic from the larger society."

Using some language other than English dooms people to second-class citizenship in American society. "Those who have the most to lose in a bilingual America," says Richard Rodriguez, "are the foreign-speaking poor." Rodriguez recalls his own boyhood: "It would have pleased me to hear my teachers address me in Spanish. . . . But I would have delayed . . . having to learn the language of public society. . . . Only when I was able to think of myself as an American, no longer an alien in *gringo* society, could I seek the rights and opportunities necessary for full public individuality."

Monolingual education opens doors to the larger world. "I didn't speak English until I was about 8 years of age," Governor Mario Cuomo recently recalled, "and there was a kind of traumatic entry into public school. It made an immense impression on me." Traumatic or not, public school taught Cuomo the most effective English among politicos of his generation.

Yet a professor at the University of Massachusetts told Rosalie Pedalino Porter, whose long experience in bilingual education led to her excellent book *Forked Tongue,* that teaching English to children reared in another language is a form of political oppression. Her rejoinder seems admirable: "When we succeed in helping our students use the majority language fluently . . . we are empowering our students rather than depriving them."

The supposed threat of bilingualism produced the campaign for a constitutional amendment making English the official language of the United States. Twenty-two states had such statutes by 1997; and in 1996 the House of Representatives actually voted for a draft amendment (after solemn discussion as to whether this would require the removal of *e pluribus unum* from American coins).

A constitutional amendment is a poor idea. Obviously all American citizens should know English. It would also be a fine thing if all American citizens knew a second language too. But English is not a language in retreat, fighting for its life, requiring drastic measures of defense. It is triumphant around the planet. Four million people spoke English in Shakespeare's time; a billion speak it now. More books are published in English than in any other language. English will be, ironically, the *lingua franca* of the twenty-first century. The notion that English needs statutory protection in the United States is a startling confession of lack of faith in the language's future. "To think that the language of Shakespeare has to have government help to survive," said one congressman, ". . . is an insult to the language." The official language campaign only creates an additional source of ethnic tension and resentment.

Nevertheless, a common language is an essential bond of cohesion in so heterogeneous a nation as America. Politicians who really care about the future of English should concentrate not on amending the Constitution but on accelerating programs to teach newcomers English. Most want to learn English as fast as they can. If they don't, their children do. But English-language classes in our great cities are swamped. Some stay open all night. According to New York's Literacy Assistance Center, 35,000 New Yorkers were enrolled in English-language programs in March 1997, while another 30,000 were on waiting lists, clamoring to get in. The pressure forces the New York Public Library to select applicants for English-language classes through a lottery.

There remains in addition the basic problem of teaching illiterates, newcomers, and citizens alike, to read and write. In 1900 the United States was the most literate nation in the world. Today the United Nations rates us forty-fifth—and in an age when literacy is more essential than ever before. Of course, expanding language programs will cost money, while demanding English as the official language only costs words. The choice between these two approaches is a good test of legislative responsibility.

III

Most ominous about the separatist impulses is the meanness generated when one group is set against another. "The chief source of man's inhumanity to man," wrote the great theologian Reinhold Niebuhr, "seems to be the tribal limits of his sense of obligation to other men." Tribal antagonisms have caused more dominating, fearing, hating, killing than any other single cause since time began.

Blacks, having suffered most grievously (at least in America) from persecution, have perhaps the greatest susceptibility to paranoia—remembering always that even paranoids may have real enemies. After all, considering what we now know about the plots against black Americans concocted by J. Edgar Hoover and executed by his FBI, who can blame blacks for being forever suspicious of white intentions?

Still, the *New York Times*–WCBS-TV poll of New Yorkers in 1990 is startling. Sixty percent of black respondents thought it true or possibly true that the government was making drugs available in black neighborhoods in order to harm black people. Twenty-nine percent thought it true or possibly true that the AIDS virus was invented by racist conspirators to kill blacks.

When Mayor Edward Koch invited the irrepressible Leonard Jeffries of CCNY to breakfast to discuss the "ice people-sun people" theory, Jeffries agreed to come "but said he would not eat because white people were trying to poison him. When he arrived," Koch reports, "I offered him coffee and danish, but he refused it. I then offered to be his food taster, but he still declined."

On another occasion, Jeffries observed that "AIDS coming out of a laboratory and finding itself localized in certain populations certainly has to be looked at as part of a conspiratorial process." After a Jeffries class, ten black students told the *Times* reporter that AIDS and drugs were indeed part of a white conspiracy. "During the Carter administration," one said, "there was a document put out that said by the year 2000, one hundred billion Africans had to be destroyed." "Because of who's being devastated the most, and growing up in the U.S. and knowing the history of slavery and racism in this country," an older black man said, "you can't be black and not feel that AIDS is some kind of experiment, some kind of plot to hit undesirable minority populations."

Nor is such speculation confined to the feverish sidewalks of New York. "Let me make a speech before a black audience," testifies William Raspberry, "and sometime during the Q & A someone is certain to ask if I believe there is a conspiracy against black Americans. It doesn't matter whether the subject is drugs or joblessness, school failure or teen pregnancy, politics or immigration. I can count on hearing some version of the conspiracy question."

The black case is only a more extreme version of the persecution complex—the feeling that someone is out to get them—to which nearly all minorities on occasion succumb. Mutual suspicion and hostility are bound to emerge in a society bent on defining itself in terms of jostling and competing groups.

IV

"The era that began with the dream of integration," Richard Rodriguez has observed, "ended up with scorn for assimilation." Instead of casting off the foreign skin, as John Quincy Adams had stipulated, never to resume it, the fashion is to resume the foreign skin as conspicuously as can be. The cult of ethnicity has reversed the movement of American history, producing a nation of minorities—or at least of minority spokesmen—less interested in joining with the majority in common endeavor than in declaring their alienation from an oppressive, white, patriarchal, racist, sexist, classist society. The ethnic ideology inculcates the illusion that membership in one or another ethnic group is the basic American experience.

Most Americans, however, continue to see themselves primarily as individuals and only secondarily and trivially as adherents of a group. Nor is harm done when ethnic groups display pride in their historic past or in their contributions to the American present. But the division of society into fixed ethnicities nourishes a culture of victimization and a contagion of inflammable sensitivities. And when a vocal and visible minority pledges primary allegiance to the group, whether ethnic, sexual, religious, or, in rare cases (communist, fascist), political, it presents a threat to the brittle bonds of national identity that hold this diverse and fractious society together.

A peculiarly ugly mood seems to have settled over the one arena where freedom of inquiry and expression should be most unconstrained and civility most respected—our colleges and universities. It is not fun running a university these days. Undergraduates can be wanton and cruel in their exclusion, their harassment, their heavy pranks, their wounding invective. Minority students, for the most understandable reasons, are often vulnerable and frightened. Racial cracks, slurs, insults, vilification pose difficult problems. Thus posters appear around the campus at the University of Michigan parodying the slogan of the United Negro College Fund: A MIND IS A TERRIBLE THING TO WASTE—ESPECIALLY ON A NIGGER. Decent white students join the protest against white bullies and thugs.

Presidents and deans begin to ask themselves, which is more important—protecting free speech or preventing racial persecution? The Constitution, Justice Holmes said, embodies "the principle of free thought—not free thought for those who agree with us but freedom for the thought that we hate." But suppose the thought we hate undercuts the Constitution's ideal of equal justice under law? Does not the First Amendment protect equality as well as liberty? how to draw a bright line between speech and behavior?

One has a certain sympathy for besieged administrators who, trying to do their best to help minority students, adopt regulations to restrict racist and sexist speech. More than a hundred institutions, according to the American Civil Liberties Union, had done so by February 1991. One can even understand why administrators, not sure what best to do for minorities and eager to keep things quiet, accept—even subsidize—separatist remedies urged by student militants. They might, however, ponder Kenneth Clark's comment: "The white liberal . . . who concedes black separatism so hastily and benevolently must look to his own reasons, not the least of them perhaps an exquisite relief." And it is sad, though instructive, that the administrations especially disposed to encourage racial and ethnic enclaves—like Berkeley, Michigan, Oberlin, the University of Massachusetts at Amherst—are, Dinesh D'Souza (himself an Indian from India) points out, the ones experiencing the most racial tension. Troy Duster, a Berkeley sociologist, finds a correlation between group separatism and racial hostility among students.

Moderates who would prefer fending for themselves as individuals are bullied into going along with their group. Groups get committed to platforms and to we-they syndromes. Faculty members appease. A code of ideological orthodoxy emerges. The code's guiding principle is that nothing should be said that might give offense to members of minority groups (and, apparently, that anything can be said that gives offense to white males of European origin).

The Office of Student Affairs at Smith College has put out a bulletin listing types of oppression for people belatedly "realizing that they are oppressed." Some samples of the Smith litany of sins:

> ABLEISM: Oppression of the differently abled by the temporarily able.

HETEROSEXISM: Oppression of those of sexual orientation other than heterosexual, such as gays, lesbians, and bisexuals; this can take place by not acknowledging their existence.

LOOKISM: The belief that appearance is an indicator of a person's value; the construction of a standard for beauty/attractiveness; and oppression through stereotypes and generalizations of both those who do not fit that standard and those who do.

Can they be kidding up there in Northampton?

The code imposes standards of what is called, now rather derisively, "political correctness." What began as a means of controlling student incivility threatens to become, formally or informally, a means of controlling curricula and faculty too. Clark University asks professors proposing courses to explain how "pluralistic (minority, women, etc.) views and concerns are explored and integrated in this course." A philosopher declined to sign, doubting that the university would ask professors to explain how "patriotic and pro-family values are explored and integrated."

Two distinguished American historians at Harvard, Bernard Bailyn and Stephan Thernstrom, offered a course in population history called "The Peopling of America." Articles appeared in the *Harvard Crimson* criticizing the professors for "racial insensitivity," and black students eventually presented them with a bill of particulars. Thernstrom, an advocate of ethnic history, the editor of the *Harvard Encyclopedia of American Eth-*

nic Groups, was accused of racism. He had, it developed, used the term "Indians" instead of "Native Americans." He had also referred to "Oriental" religion—the adjective was deemed "colonial and imperialistic." Bailyn had recommended diaries of Southern planters without recommending slave narratives. And so on, for six single-spaced pages.

The episode reminds one of the right-wing students who in Joe McCarthy days used to haunt the classrooms of liberal Harvard professors (like me) hoping to catch whiffs of Marxism emanating from the podium. Thernstrom decided to hell with it and gave up the course. A signal triumph for political correctness.

Those who stand up for what they believe invite smear campaigns. A favorite target these days is Diane Ravitch of New York University, a first-class historian of American education, an enlightened advocate of school reform, and a steadfast champion of cultural pluralism. She is dedicated to reasoned and temperate argument and is perseveringly conciliatory rather than polemical in her approach. Perhaps the fact that she is a woman persuades ethnic chauvinists that they can bully her. Despite nasty efforts at intimidation, she continues to expose the perils of ethnocentrism with calm lucidity.

Ravitch's unpardonable offense seems to be her concern about *unum* as well as about *pluribus*—her belief that history should help us understand how bonds of cohesion make us a nation rather than an irascible collection of unaffiliated groups. For in the end, the cult of ethnicity defines the republic not as a polity of individuals but as a congeries of distinct and inviolable cultures. When a student sent a memorandum to the "diversity education committee" at the University of Pennsylvania mentioning her "deep regard for the individual," a college administrator returned the paper with the word *individual* underlined: "This is a *red flag* phrase today, which is considered by many to be *racist*. Arguments that champion the individual over the group ultimately privileges [*sic*] the 'individuals' belonging to the largest or dominant group."

The contemporary sanctification of the group threatens the old idea of a coherent society. Multicultural zealots reject as hegemonic the notion of a shared commitment to common ideals. How far the discourse has come from Crèvecoeur's "new race," from Tocqueville's civic participation, from Emerson's "smelting pot," from Bryce's "amazing solvent," from Myrdal's "American Creed"!

Yet what has held the American people together in the absence of a common ethnic origin has been precisely a common adherence to ideals of democracy and human rights that, too often transgressed in practice, forever goad us to narrow the gap between practice and principle.

Plainly there is no incompatibility between fidelity to the unifying civic principles that hold us together as Americans and fidelity, if one wishes it, to any particular religious or ethnic or racial or gender group. It is a vital part of America for people to cherish their own traditions, observances, organizations, customs, rituals, holidays, parades, cuisines. It is these strands of particularity that lend richness and texture to our society.

The American synthesis has an inevitable Anglo-Saxon coloration, but it is no longer an exercise in Anglo-

Saxon domination. The republic embodies ideals that transcend ethnic, religious, and political lines. It is an experiment, reasonably successful for a while, in creating a common identity for people of diverse races, religions, languages, cultures. But the experiment can continue to succeed only so long as Americans continue to believe in the goal. If the republic now turns away from Washington's old goal of "one people," what is its future?—disintegration of the national community, apartheid, Balkanization, tribalization?

"The one absolutely certain way of bringing this nation to ruin, of preventing all possibility of its continuing to be a nation at all," said Theodore Roosevelt, "would be to permit it to become a tangle of squabbling nationalities, an intricate knot of German-Americans, Irish-Americans, English-Americans, French-Americans, Scandinavian-Americans, or Italian-Americans, each preserving its separate nationality." Three-quarters of a century later we must add a few more nationalities to T. R.'s brew. This only strengthens his point. But what was a nightmare for T. R. is the dream of multicultural ideologues today. If that dream were fulfilled, if each of our manifold groups were huddled in its own enclave, holding itself apart from the rest in the sacred name of diversity, would this really be a more equable, peaceful, strong, unified, happy country?

5

☆ ☆ ☆ ☆

E Pluribus Unum?

The attack on the common American identity is the culmination of the cult of ethnicity. That attack was mounted in the first instance by European Americans of non-British origin ("unmeltable ethnics") against the British foundations of American culture; then, latterly and massively, by Americans of non-European origin against the European foundations of that culture. As Theodore Roosevelt's foreboding suggests, the European immigration itself palpitated with internal hostilities, everyone at everybody else's throats—hardly the "monocultural" crowd portrayed by ethnocentric separatists. After all, the two great "world" wars of the twentieth century began as fights among European states. Making a single society out of this diversity of antagonistic European peoples is a hard enough job. The new salience of non-European, nonwhite stocks compounds the challenge. And the non-Europeans, or at least their self-appointed spokesmen, bring with them a resentment, in some cases a hatred, of Europe and the West provoked by generations of Western colonialism, racism, condescension, contempt, and cruel exploitation.

I

Will not this rising flow of non-European immigrants create a "minority majority" that will make Eurocentrism obsolete by the twenty-first century? This is the fear of some white Americans and the hope (and sometimes the threat) of some nonwhites.

Immigrants were responsible for a third of population growth during the 1980s. More arrived than in any decade since the second of the century. And the composition of the newcomers changed dramatically. In 1910 nearly 90 percent of immigrants came from Europe. In the 1980s more than 80 percent came from Asia and Latin America.

Still, foreign-born residents constitute less than 10 percent of the population today as against nearly 15 percent when the first Roosevelt and Wilson were worrying about hyphenated Americans. Stephan Thernstrom doubts that the minority majority will ever arrive. The

black share in the population has grown rather slowly—
9.9 percent in 1920, 10 percent in 1950, 11.1 percent in
1970, 12.1 percent in 1990. Neither Asian-Americans nor
Hispanic-Americans go in for especially large families;
and family size in any case tends to decline as income and
intermarriage increase. "If today's immigrants assimilate
to American ways as readily as their predecessors at the
turn of the century—as seems to be happening," Thernstrom concludes, "there won't be a minority majority
issue anyway."

America has so long seen itself as the asylum for the
oppressed and persecuted—and has done itself and the
world so much good thereby—that any curtailment of
immigration offends something in the American soul. No
one wants to be a Know-Nothing. Yet uncontrolled immigration is an impossibility; so the criteria of control are
questions the American democracy must confront. We
have shifted the basis of admission three times this century—from national origins in 1924 to family reunifica-
tion in 1965 to needed skills in 1990. The future of
immigration policy depends on the capacity of the assimilation process to continue to do what it has done so
well in the past: to lead newcomers to an acceptance of
the language, the institutions, and the political ideals that
hold the nation together.

II

Is Europe really the root of all evil? The crimes of
Europe against lesser breeds without the law (not to
mention even worse crimes—Hitlerism and Stalinism—

against fellow Europeans) are famous. But these crimes do not alter other facts of history: that Europe was the birthplace of the United States of America, that European ideas and culture formed the republic, that the United States is an extension of European civilization, and that nearly 80 percent of Americans are of European descent.

When Irving Howe, hardly a notorious conservative, dared write, "The Bible, Homer, Plato, Sophocles, Shakespeare are central to our culture," an outraged reader ("having graduated this past year from Amherst") wrote, "Where on Howe's list is the *Quran,* the *Gita,* Confucius, and other central cultural artifacts of the peoples of our nation?" No one can doubt the importance of these works nor the influence they have had on other societies. But on American society? It may be too bad that dead white European males have played so large a role in shaping our culture. But that's the way it is. One cannot erase history.

These humdrum historical facts, and not some dastardly imperialist conspiracy, explain the Eurocentric slant in American schools. Would anyone seriously argue that teachers should suppress the European origins of American civilization? or that schools should cater to the 20 percent and ignore the 80 percent? Of course the 20 percent and their contributions should be integrated into the curriculum too, which is the point of cultural pluralism.

But self-styled "multiculturalists" are very often ethnocentric separatists who see little in the Western heritage beyond Western crimes. The Western tradition, in this view, is inherently racist, sexist, "classist," hegemonic;

irredeemably repressive, irredeemably oppressive. The spread of Western culture is due not to any innate quality but simply to the spread of Western power. Thus the popularity of European classical music around the world—and, one supposes, of American jazz and rock too—is evidence not of inherent appeal but of "the pattern of imperialism, in which the conquered culture adopts that of the conqueror."

Such animus toward Europe lay behind the well-known crusade against the Western-civilization course at Stanford ("Hey-hey, ho-ho, Western culture's got to go!"). According to the National Endowment for the Humanities, students can graduate from 78 percent of American colleges and universities without taking a course in the history of Western civilization. A number of institutions—among them Dartmouth, Wisconsin, Mt. Holyoke—require courses in third-world or ethnic studies but not in Western civilization. The mood is one of divesting Americans of the sinful European inheritance and seeking redemptive infusions from non-Western cultures.

III

One of the oddities of the situation is that the assault on the Western tradition is conducted very largely with analytical weapons forged in the West. What are the names invoked by the coalition of latter-day Marxists, deconstructionists, poststructuralists, radical feminists, Afrocentrists? Marx, Nietzsche, Gramsci, Derrida, Foucault, Lacan, Sartre, de Beauvoir, Habermas, the Frankfurt "critical theory" school—Europeans all. The "unmasking," "demythologizing," "decanonizing," "dehegemonizing" blitz against Western culture depends on methods of critical analysis unique to the West—which surely testifies to the internally redemptive potentialities of the Western tradition.

Even Afrocentrists seem to accept subliminally the very Eurocentric standards they think they are rejecting. "Black intellectuals condemn Western civilization," Professor Pearce Williams says, "yet ardently wish to prove it was founded by their ancestors." And, like Frantz Fanon and Léopold Senghor, whose books figure prominently on their reading lists, Afrocentric ideologues are intellectual children of the West they repudiate. Fanon, the eloquent spokesman of the African wretched of the earth, had French as his native tongue and based his analyses on Freud, Marx, and Sartre. Senghor, the prophet of Negritude, wrote in French, established the Senegalese educational system on the French model and, when he left the presidency of Senegal, retired to France.

Western hegemony, it would seem, can be the source of protest as well as of power. Indeed, the invasion of American schools by the Afrocentric curriculum, not to mention the conquest of university departments of English and comparative literature by deconstructionists, poststructuralists, etc., are developments that by themselves refute the extreme theory of "cultural hegemony." Of course, Gramsci had a point. Ruling values do dominate and permeate any society; but they do not have the rigid and monolithic grip on American democracy that academic leftists claim.

Radical academics denounce the "canon" as an instrument of European oppression enforcing the hegemony of the white race, the male sex, and the capitalist class, designed, in the words of one professor, "to rewrite the past and construct the present from the perspective of the privileged and the powerful." Or in the elegant words of another—and a professor of theological ethics at that: "The canon of great literature was created by high Anglican assholes to underwrite their social class."

The poor old canon is seen not only as conspiratorial but as static. Yet nothing changes more regularly and reliably than the canon: compare, for example, the canon in American poetry as defined by Edmund Clarence Stedman in his *Poets of America* (1885) with the canon of 1935 or of 1985 (whatever happened to Longfellow and Whittier?); or recall the changes that have overtaken the canonical literature of American history in the last half-century (who reads Beard and Parrington now?). And the critics clearly have no principled objection to the idea of the canon. They simply wish to replace an old gang by a new gang. After all, a canon means only that because you can't read everything, you give some books priority over others.

Oddly enough, serious Marxists—Marx and Engels, Lukacs, Trotsky, Gramsci—had the greatest respect for what Lukacs called "the classical heritage of mankind." Well they should have, for most great literature and much good history are deeply subversive in their impact on orthodoxies. Consider the present-day American literary canon: Emerson, Jefferson, Melville, Whitman, Hawthorne, Thoreau, Lincoln, Twain, Dickinson, William and Henry James, Henry Adams, Holmes,

Dreiser, Faulkner, O'Neill. Lackeys of the ruling class? Apologists for the privileged and the powerful? Agents of American imperialism? Come on!

It is time to adjourn the chat about hegemony. If hegemony were as real as the cultural radicals pretend, Afrocentrism would never have got anywhere, and the heirs of William Lyon Phelps would still be running the Modern Language Association.

IV

Is the Western tradition a bar to progress and a curse on humanity? Would it really do America and the world good to get rid of the European legacy?

No doubt Europe has done terrible things, not least to itself. But what culture has not? History, said Edward Gibbon, is little more than the register of the crimes, follies, and misfortunes of mankind. The sins of the West are no worse than the sins of Asia or of the Middle East or of Africa.

There remains, however, a crucial difference between the Western tradition and the others. Unlike other cultures, the West has conceived and acted upon ideals that expose and combat its own misdeeds. No other culture has built self-criticism into the very fabric of its being. The crimes of the West in time generated their own antidotes. They have provoked great movements to end slavery, to raise the status of women, to abolish torture, to combat racism, to promote religious tolerance, to defend freedom of inquiry and expression, to advance personal liberty and human rights.

Whatever the particular crimes of Europe, that continent is also the source—the *unique* source—of those liberating ideas of individual liberty, political democracy, equality before the law, freedom of worship, human rights, and cultural freedom that constitute our most precious legacy and to which most of the world today aspires. These are *European* ideas, not Asian, nor African, nor Middle Eastern ideas, except by adoption.

The freedoms of inquiry and of artistic creation, for example, are Western values. Consider the differing reactions to the case of Salman Rushdie: what the West saw as an intolerable attack on individual freedom the Middle East saw as a proper punishment for an evildoer who had violated the mores of his group. Individualism itself is looked on with abhorrence and dread by collectivist cultures in which loyalty to the group overrides personal goals—cultures that, social scientists say, comprise about 70 percent of the world's population.

There is surely no reason for Western civilization to have guilt trips laid on it by champions of cultures based on despotism, superstition, tribalism, and fanaticism. In this regard the Afrocentrists are especially absurd. The West needs no lectures on the superior virtue of those "sun people" who sustained slavery until Western imperialism abolished it (and sustain it to this day in Mauritania and the Sudan), who keep women in subjection, marry several at once, and mutilate their genitals, who carry out racial persecutions not only against Indians and other Asians but against fellow Africans from the wrong tribes, who show themselves either incapable of operating a democracy or ideologically hostile to the democratic idea, and who in their tyrannies and massacres, their

Idi Amins and Boukassas, have stamped with utmost brutality on human rights. Keith B. Richburg, a black newspaperman who served for three years as the *Washington Post*'s bureau chief in Africa, saw bloated bodies floating down a river in Tanzania from the insanity that was Rwanda and thought: "There but for the grace of God go I. . . . Thank God my nameless ancestor, brought across the ocean in chains and leg irons, made it out alive. . . . Thank God I am an American."

Certainly the European overlords did little enough to prepare Africa for self-government. But democracy would find it hard in any case to put down roots in a tribalist and patrimonial culture that, long before the West invaded Africa, had sanctified the personal authority of chieftains and ordained the obedience of the tribe. What the West would call corruption is regarded through much of Africa as no more than the prerogative of power. Competitive political parties, an independent judiciary, a free press, the rule of law are alien to African traditions.

It was the French, not the Algerians, who freed Algerian women from the veil (much to the irritation of Frantz Fanon, who regarded deveiling as symbolic rape); as in India it was the British, not the Indians, who ended (or did their best to end) the horrible custom of *suttee*—widows burning themselves alive on their husbands' funeral pyres. And it was the West, not the non-Western cultures, that launched the crusade to abolish slavery—and in doing so encountered mighty resistance, especially in the Islamic world (where Moslems, with fine impartiality, enslaved whites as well as blacks). Those many brave and humane Africans who are struggling these days for decent societies are animated by Western, not by African, ideals. White guilt can be pushed too far.

The Western commitment to human rights has unquestionably been intermittent and imperfect. Yet the ideal remains—and movement toward it has been real, if sporadic. Today it is the *Western* democratic tradition that attracts and empowers people of all continents, creeds, and colors. When the Chinese students cried and died for democracy in Tiananmen Square, they brought with them not representations of Confucius or Buddha but a model of the Statue of Liberty.

V

The great American asylum, as Crèvecoeur called it, open, as Washington said, to the oppressed and persecuted of all nations, has been from the start an experiment in a multiethnic society. This is a bolder experiment than we sometimes remember. History is littered with the wreck of states that tried to combine diverse ethnic or linguistic or religious groups within a single sovereignty. Today's headlines tell of imminent crisis or impending dissolution in one or another multiethnic polity. The luck so far of the American experiment has been due in large part to the vision of the melting pot. "No other nation," Margaret Thatcher has said, "has so successfully combined people of different races and nations within a single culture."

But even in the United States, ethnic ideologues have not been without effect. They set themselves against the old American ideal of assimilation. They call on the republic to think in terms not of individual but of group identity and to move the polity from individual rights to group rights. They have made a certain progress in transforming the United States into a more segregated society. They have done their best to turn a college generation against Europe and the Western tradition. The Afrocentric and bilingual curricula they would impose on the public schools are well designed to exclude minority children from the American mainstream. They tell minority groups that the Western democratic tradition is not for them. They encourage minorities to see themselves as victims and to live by alibis rather than to claim the opportunities opened for them by the potent combination of minority protest and white guilt. They fill the air with recrimination and rancor and have remarkably advanced the fragmentation of American life.

Yet I believe the campaign against the idea of common ideals and a single society will fail. Gunnar Myrdal was surely right: for all the damage it has done, the upsurge of ethnicity is a superficial enthusiasm stirred by romantic ideologues and unscrupulous hucksters whose claim to speak for their minorities is thoughtlessly accepted by the media. I doubt that the ethnic vogue expresses a yearning for apartheid among the minorities themselves. Indeed, the more the ideologues press the case for ethnic separatism, the less they appeal to the mass of their own groups. They have thus far done better in intimidating the white majority than in converting their own constituencies.

"No nation in history," writes Lawrence Fuchs, the political scientist and immigration expert in his fine book

The American Kaleidoscope, "had proved as successful as the United States in managing ethnic diversity. No nation before had ever made diversity itself a source of national identity and unity." The second sentence explains the success described in the first, and the mechanism for translating diversity into unity has been the American Creed, the civic culture—the very assimilating, unifying culture that is today challenged, and not seldom rejected, by the ideologues of ethnicity.

A historian's guess is that the resources of the Creed have not been exhausted. Americanization has not lost its charms. Many sons and daughters of ethnic neighborhoods still want to shed their ethnicity and move to the suburbs as fast as they can—where they will be received with far more tolerance than they would have been 70 years ago. Others may enjoy their ethnic neighborhoods but see no conflict between foreign descent and American loyalty. Unlike the multiculturalists, they celebrate not only what is distinctive in their own backgrounds but what they hold in common with the rest of the population. The desire for achievement and success in American society remains a potent force for assimilation. Gunnar Myrdal's assessment still holds true today: "The minority peoples of the United States are fighting for status in the larger society; the minorities of Europe are mainly fighting for independence from it."

The ethnic identification often tends toward superficiality. The sociologist Richard Alba's study of children and grandchildren of immigrants in the Albany, New York, area shows the most popular "ethnic experience" to be sampling the ancestral cuisine. Still, less than half the respondents picked that, and only one percent ate ethnic food every day. Only one-fifth acknowledged a sense of special relationship to people of their own ethnic background; less than one-sixth taught their children about their ethnic origins; almost none was fluent in the language of the old country. "It is hard to avoid the conclusion," Alba writes, "that ethnic experience is shallow for the great majority of whites."

If ethnic experience is a good deal less shallow for blacks, it is because of their bitter life in America, not because of nostalgia for Africa. Yet even black Americans, who have the strongest reasons for cynicism and despair, fight bravely and patriotically for their country, would move to the suburbs if income and racism would permit, and riot in the inner city not because they want separatism but because they want the same amenities and opportunities as white Americans.

As for Hispanic-Americans, first-generation Hispanics born in the United States speak English fluently, according to a Rand Corporation study; more than half of second-generation Hispanics give up Spanish altogether. A 1996 survey reported that among five educational goals, 51 percent of Hispanic parents regarded learning English as most important as against 11 percent for Spanish and 4 percent for "learning about Hispanic culture." Asked how soon Hispanic-American children should be taught English, 63 percent said as soon as possible; only 17 percent felt their children should be taught Spanish first. When PEN, the international organization of writers, held a Latino Literature Festival in New York, the Latino writers concluded: "We didn't want any more 'barrioization.' We are, we declared, American writers." When *Vista*, an English-language monthly for Hispanics,

asked its readers what historical figures they most ad-
mired, Washington, Lincoln, and Theodore Roosevelt
led the list, with Benito Juárez trailing as fourth, and
Eleanor Roosevelt and Martin Luther King, Jr., tied for
fifth. So much for ethnic role models. Latinos are the
most recent wave of immigrants and also those who can
most easily return to their homelands. Yet the majority
aspire to be Americans first.

Professor Andrew Hacker, author of a valuable and
admonitory book *Two Nations: Black and White, Separate, Hostile, Unequal,* remarks about the children of new
immigrants in his classes at Queens College in New York
City: "The vast majority of immigrant parents intend to
stay and see their children become fully-fledged Americans. . . . Hardly any of these parents are pressing for
multicultural textbooks, or to have their particular nationalities written into the lessons. Their dream is to have
their sons and daughters do well."

What is even more fatal to identity politics and the
cult of ethnicity is the simple fact that many, probably
most, Americans are of mixed ancestry. They do not see
themselves as belonging to a single ethnic group. And
the mix is growing every day. The wedding notices in any
newspaper testify to the equanimity with which people
marry people of different ancestry, religion, and race. So
many Jewish-Americans marry outside their faith that
Jewish leaders worry about the future of the American
Jewish community. More Japanese-Americans marry
Caucasians than they do other Japanese-Americans. Over
seventy percent of American Indians marry non-Indians.
Black-white marriages, banned in nineteen states until
the Supreme Court banned the bans in 1967, have risen

from 2.6 percent of all marriages by blacks in 1970 to 12.1 percent in 1993 and continue to rise each passing year.

The multicultural enthusiasm has encouraged the classification of Americans for census or affirmative action purposes into ethnic and racial categories. But the mixing process has in its turn led to protests by multi-ethnic Americans who insist on their right to reject particularist identities. In 1996 thousands of mixed-race Americans joined the Multiracial Solidarity March in Washington to press the government to add a multiracial category to the 2000 census.

Whatever the Census Bureau eventually does, the mixing process will continue. Derek Walcott, condemning Europe's ethnic cleansing in his 1993 Nobel Prize lecture, spoke of lands where "citizens would intermarry as they chose, from instinct, not tradition, until their children find it increasingly futile to trace their genealogy." America is more and more that way. Tiger Woods—one-fourth Thai, one-fourth Chinese, one-fourth black, one-eighth white, and one-eighth American Indian—foreshadows the future. We can, I am sure, count on the power of sex—and of love—to defeat those who would seek to divide the country into separate ethnic communities.

VI

The ethnic revolt against the melting pot has reached the point, in rhetoric at least, though not I think in reality, of a denial of the idea of a common culture and a single society. If large numbers of people really accept this, the republic would be in serious trouble.

"For thirty years," the historian John Higham writes, "nation-building virtually disappeared from the agenda of academic historians," and he calls on scholars to "take seriously the construction of national and universal as well as ethnic, racial, and particularistic loyalties." "In the excitement of discovering how much there was to learn about the experiences of peoples formerly excluded from the historical record," writes the western historian Patricia Nelson Limerick, "we have backed away from any vision of human ground; we have, instead, divided American life into a set of experiences. . . . Did we, by virtue of that emphasis, unintentionally cut some of the ground under empathy, compassion, fellow feeling, and understanding? Might it be time to build some of that foundation back in?"

The question poses itself: how to build back that foundation? How to restore the balance between *unum* and *pluribus*? The old American homogeneity disappeared well over a century ago, never to return. Ever since, we have been preoccupied in one way or another with the problem, as Herbert Croly phrased in 80 years back in *The Promise of American Life,* "of preventing such divisions from dissolving the society into which they enter—of keeping such a highly differentiated society fundamentally sound and whole." This required, Croly believed, an "ultimate bond of union." There was only one way by which solidarity could be restored, "and that is by means of a democratic social ideal."

The genius of America lies in its capacity to forge a single nation from peoples of remarkably diverse racial, religious, and ethnic origins. It has done so because democratic principles provide both the philosophical bond of union and practical experience in civic participation. The American Creed envisages a nation composed of individuals making their own choices and accountable to themselves, not a nation based on inviolable ethnic communities. The Constitution turns on individual rights, not on group rights. Law, in order to rectify past wrongs, has from time to time (and in my view often properly so) acknowledged the claims of groups; but this is the exception, not the rule.

Our democratic principles contemplate an open society founded on tolerance of differences and on mutual respect. In practice, America has been more open to some than to others. But it is more open to all today than it was yesterday and is likely to be even more open tomorrow than today. The persistent movement of American life has been from exclusion to inclusion.

Historically and culturally this republic has an Anglo-Saxon base; but from the start the base has been modified, enriched, and reconstituted by transfusions from other continents and civilizations. The movement from exclusion to inclusion causes a constant revision in the texture of our culture. The ethnic transfusions affect all aspects of American life—our politics, our literature, our music, our painting, our movies, our cuisine, our customs, our dreams. Black Americans in particular have influenced the ever-changing national culture in many ways. "Not since ancient Rome conquered and then sur-

rendered to the culture of its Greek slaves and freedmen," observes Orlando Patterson, "has the culture of a
dominant world civilization been so enormously influenced by so small a minority of people."

Black Americans have lived here for centuries, and,
unless one believes in racist mysticism, they belong far
more to American culture than to the culture of Africa.
Their history is part of the Western democratic tradition,
not an alternative to it. Henry Louis Gates Jr., reminds us
of James Baldwin's remark about coming to Europe to
find out that he was "as American as any Texas G.I." No
one does black Americans more disservice than those
Afrocentric ideologues who would define them out of
the West.

It is only in the last half century that white America
has begun to acknowledge and confront the racism that
has disfigured the national past. Only in the last half century have white Americans finally grown conscious of the
racial oppression practiced so unconsciously for the
greater part of American history—practiced at the expense of the ideal of equality enshrined in our sacred
documents.

Progress has been made and cannot be denied. If
anyone had told me half a century ago that in my lifetime,
with black Americans only twelve percent of the population, I would see a black general as chairman of the Joint
Chiefs of Staff, black justices on the Supreme Court, a
black governor of Virginia, black mayors of Atlanta,
Birmingham, New Orleans, and other southern cities (as
well as of New York, Chicago, Washington, Los Angeles,
Philadelphia, Detroit, Seattle, St. Louis, Kansas City),

not to mention blacks playing in the major leagues, I would have been happy but incredulous. Yet all this has taken place.

Why then do some observers believe that relations between the races are getting worse? The great Tocqueville answered that question a century and a half ago. Explaining why in the years before the French Revolution those parts of France that had enjoyed most improvement also exhibited most discontent, Tocqueville wrote, "It is not always when things are going from bad to worse that revolutions break out. . . . Patiently endured so long as it seemed beyond redress, a grievance comes to appear intolerable once the possibility of removing it crosses men's minds. For the mere fact that certain abuses have been remedied draws attention to the others and they now appear more galling; people may suffer less, but their sensibility is exacerbated." So improvements in people's lot may at the same time quicken the spirit of protest.

"The sociological truths," writes Orlando Patterson, "are that America, while still flawed in its race relations . . . , is now the least racist white-majority society in the world; has a better record of legal protection of minorities than any other society, white or black; offers more opportunities to a greater number of black persons than any other society, including all those of Africa; and has gone through a dramatic change in its attitude toward miscegenation over the past 25 years."

The interplay of diverse traditions produces the America we know. "Paradoxical though it may seem," Diane Ravitch has well said, "the United States has a common culture that is multicultural." That is why unifying political ideals coexist so easily and cheerfully with diversity in social and cultural values. Within the overarching political commitment, people are free to live as they choose, ethnically and otherwise. Differences will remain; some are reinvented; some are used to drive us apart. But as we renew our allegiance to the unifying ideals, we provide the solvent that will prevent differences from escalating into antagonism and hatred.

One powerful reason for the movement from exclusion to inclusion is that the American Creed facilitates the appeal from the actual to the ideal. When we talk of the American democratic faith, we must understand it in its true dimensions. It is not an impervious, final, and complacent orthodoxy, intolerant of deviation and dissent, fulfilled in flag salutes, oaths of allegiance, and hands over the heart. It is an ever-evolving philosophy, fulfilling its ideals through debate, self-criticism, protest, disrespect, and irreverence; a tradition in which all have rights of heterodoxy and opportunities for self-assertion. The Creed has been the means by which Americans have haltingly but persistently narrowed the gap between performance and principle. It is what all Americans should learn, because it is what binds all Americans together.

Let us by all means in this increasingly mixed-up world learn about those other continents and civilizations. But let us master our own history first. Lamentable as some may think it, we inherit an American experience, as America inherits a European experience. To deny the essentially European origins of American culture is to falsify history.

Americans of whatever origin should take pride in

the distinctive inheritance to which they have all contributed, as other nations take pride in their distinctive inheritances. Belief in one's own culture does not require disdain for other cultures. But one step at a time: no culture can hope to ingest other cultures all at once, certainly not before it ingests its own. As we begin to master our own culture, then we can explore the world.

Our schools and colleges have a responsibility to teach history for its own sake—as part of the intellectual equipment of civilized persons—and not to degrade history by allowing its contents to be dictated by pressure groups, whether ideological, economic, religious, or ethnic. The past may sometimes offend one or another group; that is no reason for rewriting history. Giving pressure lobbies vetoes over textbooks and courses betrays both history and education. Properly taught, history will convey a sense of the variety, continuity, and adaptability of cultures, of the need for understanding other cultures, of the ability of individuals and peoples to overcome obstacles, of the importance of critical analysis and dispassionate judgment in every area of life.

Above all, history can give a sense of national identity. We don't have to believe that our values are absolutely better than the next fellow's or the next country's, but we have no doubt that they are better *for us,* reared as we are—and are worth living by and worth dying for. For our values are not matters of whim and happenstance. History has given them to us. They are anchored in our national experience, in our great national documents, in our national heroes, in our folkways, traditions, and standards. People with a different history will have differing values. But we believe that our own are better for us. They work for us; and, for that reason, we live and die by them.

It has taken time to make the values real for all our citizens, and we still have a good distance to go, but we have made progress. If we now repudiate the quite marvelous inheritance that history bestows on us, we invite the fragmentation of the national community into a quarrelsome spatter of enclaves, ghettos, tribes. The bonds of cohesion in our society are sufficiently fragile, or so it seems to me, that it makes no sense to strain them by encouraging and exalting cultural and linguistic apartheid.

The American identity will never be fixed and final; it will always be in the making. Changes in the population have always brought changes in the national ethos and will continue to do so; but not, one must hope, at the expense of national integration. The question America confronts as a pluralistic society is how to vindicate cherished cultures and traditions without breaking the bonds of cohesion—common ideals, common political institutions, common language, common culture, common fate—that hold the republic together.

Our task is to combine due appreciation of the splendid diversity of the nation with due emphasis on the great unifying Western ideas of individual freedom, political democracy, and human rights. These are the ideas that define the American nationality—and that today empower people of all continents, races, and creeds.

"What then is the American, this new man? . . . Here individuals of all nations are melted into a new race of men." Still a good answer—still the best hope.

Epilogue

☆ ☆ ☆ ☆

MULTICULTURALISM, MONOCULTURALISM, AND THE BILL OF RIGHTS: UPDATE ON THE CULTURE WARS

Culture *wars*? The military metaphor may be a bit melodramatic; but for a decade these so-called wars have indeed agitated the American educational scene, remolding curriculums, revising canons, perplexing administrators, infuriating alumni, and otherwise disturbing the peace.

The immediate cause of this turbulence, as we have seen, is the challenge of "multiculturalism"—a neologism that suddenly invaded public discussion. It is odd that the word should be new, since the United States has been from birth a multicultural nation. But through most of American history what we now term multiculturalism had been regarded as merely a stage in the absorption of newcomers into a common American nationality and culture.

Recently multiculturalism has emerged not alone as a word but as an ideology and a mystique. In its mild form, it calls attention to neglected groups, themes, and viewpoints and redresses a shameful imbalance in the treatment of minorities both in the actualities of life and in the judgments of history. It does this within a conception of a shared culture.

However, multiculturalism also assumes a militant form in which it opposes the idea of a common culture, rejects the goals of assimilation and integration, and celebrates the immutability of diverse and separate ethnic and racial communities. Extreme separationists, while often flourishing the multicultural flag, in fact rush beyond true multiculturalism into ethnocentrism, the belief in the superior virtue of their own ethnic group.

Militant multiculturalism and ethnocentrism are fueled by understandable historic resentments. Though the American theory opens citizenship to all who subscribe to the Constitution and the laws, American practice was long confined and circumscribed. Non-Anglo-Saxon whites were snubbed and shunned. Most black Americans were slaves until 1865. Women could not vote until 1920.

But if practice betrayed theory in the short run, in the longer run theory has modified practice. The movement from exclusion to inclusion, uneven but persevering, is one of the grand themes of American history. This is what has enabled a miscellany of polyglot peoples to form a single nation. Yet militant multiculturalists, instead of recognizing the beauty of *e pluribus unum,* prefer to dismiss *unum* and exalt *pluribus.*

All this comes at a time when the murderous disintegration of one country after another around the globe gives new urgency to the question: what holds a nation together? "We look with some mixture of sadness and superiority," writes William Raspberry, "at the breakup of the Soviet Union and Yugoslavia into ethnic enclaves and fail to see how fragmented a society we in the United States are becoming. . . . We are abandoning even the *myth* that we are all Americans. . . . We are not yet as ethnically riven as, say, Yugoslavia. But don't ever imagine that it couldn't happen here."

Maybe it could happen here, but, as noted earlier, sex and love provide a potent antidote. And strong counterstatements to disuniting multiculturalism have appeared in recent writings by the political scientists Lawrence Fuchs and Peter Salins, the historians Philip Gleason, John Higham, and David Hollinger, the sociologist Todd Gitlin and the journalists Bill Raspberry, Stanley Crouch, Jim Sleeper, William Pfaff, and Richard Bernstein. The debate roars on, and it may be of interest to take a look at issues that have acquired new salience.

I

Identity politics has produced a bizarre exchange of positions between the traditional right and the traditional left. Historically the right has been particularist, affirming the complex density of life, venerating established institutions, disdaining glittering generalities. Historically the left has been universalist, embracing all humanity in broad abstractions and spacious dreams. But the cult of ethnicity has given the left a direction that, in the view of radicals of an older school, threatens not only the disuniting of nations but the disuniting of the left itself.

In Great Britain the brilliant Marxist historian Eric Hobsbawm condemns identity politics for its reduction of the left to a coalition of self-centered minority groups and interests. The political project of the left, Hobsbawm writes, should be "for *all* human beings. However we interpret the words, it isn't liberty for shareholders or blacks, but for everybody. It isn't equality for members of the Garrick Club or the handicapped, but for everybody. It is not fraternity only for old Etonians or gays, but for everybody." The identity groups, however, "are about themselves, for themselves, and nobody else. . . . That is why the Left cannot *base* itself on identity groups."

In the United States Todd Gitlin, a 1960s activist before he turned sociologist, similarly deplores what he calls "the twilight of common dreams." In the past the left affirmed the broad human condition and the equal-

ity of all persons; it was the right that rested on primor-
dial differences among classes, nations, races. Liberal
politicians used to put together balanced tickets to create
majority coalitions for general objectives; the old ethnic
politics was a force for social cohesion. The new ethnic
politics, Gitlin points out, is obsessed with group difference and inculcates thereby a "go-it-alone mood," every
tribe for itself.

The result? "Today it is the Right that speaks a language of commonalities. . . . To be on the Left, meanwhile, is to doubt that one can speak of humanity at all."
Gitlin may overdo the enthusiasm of the right for universalist values, but he is surely correct in his argument
that the cult of ethnicity has confused and enfeebled the
left. Even the Democratic party suffered for a period
from a plague of institutionalized "caucuses" represent-
ing minorities concerned more with ventilating their own
grievances than with strengthening the party.

II

Identity politics has produced another bizarre effect. The
Bill of Rights is once more in peril, especially its corner-
stone, the First Amendment, that cherished guardian of
our freedoms of speech, press, worship, assembly, and
petition. In the good old days the First Amendment was
a target of attack by the right. Conservatives and hyperpatriots were the ardent advocates of repression and censorship. Many still are, but today they are joined in the
assault on the First Amendment by identity groups on
the left. Even more ironically, the rising demand for re-

pression and censorship is centered in our universities—
the places above all where unlimited freedom of expression had previously been deemed sacred. And those who
now lead the assault on the Bill of Rights do so in the
name of the multicultural society.

The reach of the First Amendment has been
widened through the years by the process of "incorpora-
tion," and the widening has been saluted, especially in
academic circles, as one of the glories of American jurisprudence. Recall some of the noble phrases that have
confirmed, strengthened, and extended freedoms of expression. "The question in every case," said Justice
Holmes, "is whether the words are used in such circumstances and are of such a nature as to create a clear and
present danger that they will bring about the substan-
tive evils that Congress has a right to prevent." "No danger flowing from speech," said Justice Brandeis, "can be
deemed clear and present, unless the incidence of evil
apprehended is so imminent that it may befall before
there is opportunity for full discussion. If there be time
to expose through discussion the falsehood and fallacies,
to avert the evil by processes of education, the remedy to
be applied is more speech, not enforced silence." I have
earlier quoted Justice Holmes's point that freedom
means not just "free thought for those who agree with
us"—what great virtue resides in that?—"but freedom
for the thought that we hate."

Freedom for the thought that we hate: this is the
proposition that now falls under attack from a multicultural perspective. Through most of the twentieth century, the thought that we hated was totalitarian political
thought: fascism, Nazism, communism. Many argued

then that free speech should not be permitted to become the means of destroying the freedom of speech; that liberty should be denied to those who would use liberty to crush liberty. Under pressure, first of hot war, then of cold war, the Supreme Court gave ground from time to time in construing First Amendment protection of hateful ideological utterance. But in the main the Bill of Rights survived hot and cold wars intact.

Thus in the midst of the Second World War, at a time of the highest patriotic fervor with the life of the nation truly at risk, the Court threw out as a violation of the First Amendment a West Virginia statute requiring school children to salute and pledge allegiance to the American flag. "Freedom to differ," Justice Jackson wrote for the Court, "is not limited to things that do not matter much. That would be a mere shadow of freedom. The test of its substance is the right to differ as to things that touch the heart of the existing order."

Justice Jackson memorably continued; "If there be any fixed star in our constitutional constellation, it is that no official, high or petty, can prescribe what shall be orthodox in politics, nationalism, religion, or other matters of opinion. . . . If there are any circumstances which permit an exception, they do not now occur to us." Alas, they now occur to the practitioners of identity politics. But the Court handed down its decision against compulsory flag salutes and pledges of allegiance on Flag Day in 1943 when young Americans were fighting and dying for that flag on many fronts around the planet; and the American people then, far from denouncing the Court, applauded the decision as a pretty good statement of what we were fighting for.

Through the Cold War, the Court generally held the line for the First Amendment. In *Brandenburg* v. *Ohio,* it reaffirmed and reformulated Holmes's clear and present danger test. In the *Skokie* case, it upheld the right of neo-Nazis to parade down the streets of an Illinois town inhabited by Holocaust survivors and their families. Wounded feelings were not deemed a persuasive reason for cancelling constitutional protection. As Justice Brennan wrote in *Texas* v. *Johnson,* a case in which a protestor burned an American flag: "If there is a bedrock principle underlying the First Amendment, it is that the government may not prohibit the expression of an idea simply because society finds the idea itself offensive or disagreeable."

III

This is the interpretation of the Bill of Rights that champions of identity politics are determined to overthrow. The account by Henry Louis Gates, Jr., of a black reaction applies also to other identity groups: "Civil liberties are regarded by many as a chief obstacle to civil rights. . . . The byword among many black activists and black intellectuals is no longer the political imperative to protect free speech; it is the moral imperative to suppress 'hate speech.' "

The very term "hate speech" is new. It does not appear as a concept or even as an index entry in Leonard Levy's *Encyclopedia of the American Constitution* (1986) or in M. Glenn Abernethy's *Civil Liberties under the*

Constitution (1989) or in Kermit E. Hall's *Oxford Companion to the Supreme Court* (1992). Nor does the related term "political correctness" make it either as a concept or as an index entry in those useful works.

Now free speech is not an absolute. We regulate speech every day through statutes punishing libel, slander, perjury, false advertising, criminal solicitation, and so on. No judgment can escape the balancing of competing values. But in a free democracy the presumption must always lie in favor of the freedom of speech unless an overwhelming practical case can be made for regulation and censorship.

The elevation of hate speech carries with it a new view of the Constitution. The traditional understanding has been that the Constitution is a charter for individuals and that the Bill of Rights adds further specific protection for individuals. But identity politics regards groups rather than individuals as the basic constitutional units and would thereby curtail individual rights in order to protect group rights. Thus Professor Kathryn Abrams of the Cornell Law School deplores "the constitutional habit of considering rights-bearers as unaffiliated individuals." She contends that "expression is overprotected" in the United States and that "we need limits on free expression in intellectual life" in order to enhance "respect for and recognition of politically marginalized groups."

Impressed by the phenomenon of Nazi anti-Semitism, the Supreme Court had a brief fling with the concept of "group libel" during and after the Second World War. But its favorable judgment (by a 5-to-4 vote) in *Beauharnais* v. *Illinois* (1952) was effectively nullified in subsequent decisions. Nor have Congress and state legislatures elected to follow the group libel path. After all, the theory of the Constitution as the palladium not of individual but of group rights rejects the American conception of civil liberties so powerfully argued by Holmes, Brandeis, Jackson, and Brennan.

Yet the group-rights theory is driven by anguished emotions—the emotions of Holocaust survivors in Skokie, the emotions of women long subjected to harassment and abuse, the emotions of blacks spurned and humiliated, the emotions of all denigrated and persecuted minorities. Democratic governments, with memories of the Holocaust and apprehensions about growing ethnic tensions, are understandably and honorably concerned to arrest the spread of ethnic and racial hatred. The United Nations led the way with the International Convention on the Elimination of All Forms of Racial Discrimination (1966) calling on signatories to declare as "an offence punishable by law all dissemination of ideas based on racial superiority, or hatred."

Various nations have followed the group-rights course. One can understand why Germany, in the light of its own horrid past, defines neo-Nazis and Holocaust deniers as clear and present dangers and takes action to ban them. But western countries with secure democratic traditions have also adopted laws punishing (I quote the British Racial Relations Act of 1965) the circulation of materials fomenting "hatred against any section of the public in Great Britain distinguished by color, race, ethnic or national origins," including "threatening, abusive, or insulting" words. Section 319 of Canada's criminal code is similarly designed to prohibit hate propaganda directed against racial and religious groups. Many democratic countries have similar statutes.

IV

Such precedents reinforce the argument for censorship of hate speech in the United States. The problem acquires peculiar poignancy in educational settings. Does not the protection of indefensible speech prevent minority students from joining the life of the university on equal terms? Does not hate speech, by subverting equality, undercut the very premises of education? Does not the Constitution protect equality as well as liberty? Is not the Fourteenth Amendment as much a part of the Constitution as the First? "The law of equality and the law of freedom of speech," writes Catharine MacKinnon, "are on a collision course in this country."

This line of argument appeals to harassed administrators and promotes the institutionalization of identity politics through speech codes, monitoring of lectures, toleration of destruction of college newspapers, even surveillance of informal conversations (including jokes)— all diminishing the zone of free and unihibited comment.

The obsession with "insensitivity"—the feeling that it is OK to ban words when they hurt someone's feelings—is a major source of the attack on the First Amendment. Unquestionably verbal slurs and insults by campus bullies can upset and intimidate defenseless individuals. But is the injury words inflict on sensibilities sufficiently weighty and enduring to require so drastic a remedy as a contraction of the First Amendment? Surely there are many ways short of censorship by which educational leaders can discourage and condemn bigotry.

The hurt-feelings standard can be carried a little far. When Henry Louis Gates, Jr., dared characterize Afrocentrism as a " 'voodoo' methodology," fourteen scholars, led by the chairs of the department of anthropology at Johns Hopkins, of the department of religion at Trinity, and of the department of black studies at the University of Massachusetts, earnestly rebuked him as "grossly insensitive" on the ground that his comment "debases the religious beliefs and practices of millions" of voodoo worshippers. They even compared him to George Bush.

At the end of this insensitivity road lie the Ayatollah Khomeini and *The Satanic Verses.* Does the fact that *The Satanic Verses* hurts the feelings of fundamentalist Muslims really justify the *fatwa,* the sentence of death pronounced against Salman Rushdie? Bernard Shaw said, "All great truths begin as blasphemies." The hurt-feelings standard, if imposed in the past, would have silenced Mark Twain, Ambrose Bierce, Mr. Dooley, H. L. Mencken, and so many others whose scorching wit has enlivened, illuminated, and improved American life.

In any case, how successful have anti-racist statutes been in stopping the dissemination of racist ideas? In Germany racist graffiti and harassment of Jews, homosexuals, and foreigners have increased. Britain reports no diminution in racism. In Canada, feminists, wielding the legal theories of Catharine MacKinnon, rejoiced when the Canadian Supreme Court affirmed the power of the state to ban literary and visual expression that "degrades" and "dehumanizes" women. But the main consequence has been the seizure by Canadian customs of books ordered by lesbian bookshops. Neither the European nor the Canadian experience demonstrates that censorship is more effective than free discussion in bringing about a tolerant and harmonious society.

When hate speech leads on to physical assault and violence, that is another matter and one requiring prompt and sharp counteraction. But plenty of existing statutes deal with violent crime. And it may well be a good idea to provide for the enhancement of punishment when hate is demonstrably the motive for violence. But driving *thoughts* underground may only cause them to explode later.

Moreover, the censorship of racist expression might well create precedents for future censorship of other sorts of expression. Some multiculturalists brush aside this point on the ground that freedom of speech is over-rated as a boon for minorities. "African-Americans and other people of color," Professor Charles Lawrence, then of the Stanford Law School, has written, "are skeptical about the argument that even the most injurious speech must remain unregulated because, in an unregulated marketplace of ideas, the best ones will rise to the top. Experience tells quite the opposite. People of color have seen too many demagogues elected by appealing to America's racism."

One wonders where Professor Lawrence has been over the last half century. Experience tells on the contrary that, in the unregulated marketplace of ideas, talk of "white supremacy" has vanished and the idea of racial equality has been accepted in principle, if not, alas, in practice. It was precisely the First Amendment, Henry Louis Gates, Jr., reminds us, that "licensed the protests, the rallies, the organization and the agitation that galvanized the nation." There are few better arguments for the Bill of Rights than the revolution in race relations over the last half century.

No one needs the First Amendment more than those who seek to change society. Radicals are always in the minority, and minorities gain most from the protections of the Bill of Rights. Free speech may at times be offensive, odious, repulsive, an instrument of domination and oppression; but historically free speech has been far more significant as a means—no, *the* means—of liberation. As Norman Corwin, whom the more venerable will remember as the author half a century ago of that once celebrated radio program on the Bill of Rights called "We Hold These Truths," recently put it: "The Bill of Rights doesn't offer freedom *from* speech. To silence an idea because it might offend a minority doesn't protect that minority. It deprives it of the tool it needs most—the right to talk back."

There is no more self-emasculating position for reformers than the curtailment of debate and expression. And the censorship strategy, on top of everything else, hands the free speech issue to the right, casts racists as champions of the First Amendment, and diverts attention from the poison they spew.

It is ironic that what the multiculturalists began as a joyous celebration of diversity ends as a grim crusade for conformity.

V

The left has no monopoly on political correctness—and this should lead prudent multiculturalists to question even further the wisdom of the censorship strategy. "The censor," Louis Menand sagely observes, "always rings twice." The right has its own version of political correctness; and, if political correctness becomes the rule, the right can turn out far larger crowds for monoculturalism than the left can for multiculturalism.

The monoculturalists are hyperpatriots, fundamentalists, evangelicals, laissez-faire doctrinaires, homophobes, anti-abortionists, pro-assault-gun people, and other zealots. They inveigh against ideas and books they deem blasphemous, atheistic, socialistic, secular humanistic, pornographic, and/or un-American and seek to impose on the hapless young their own pinched, angry, monistic concept of America.

Leftwing political correctness is more systematically thought out and more pretentious in its rationalization. It concentrates its corrective program on institutions of higher education. Rightwing political correctness is more primitive and more emotional. It concentrates its corrective program on public schools, public libraries, local newspapers, and local radio and television stations.

Leftwing political correctness is an irritation and a nuisance. It becomes a threat to the young only when it invades the public schools, as indeed it has done in its Afrocentric guise in several of our cities. So long as it operates in higher education, it runs up against students who are mature enough to take care of themselves and, if not mature, are hard to persuade of anything anyway.

Rightwing political correctness catches kids before they are old enough to take care of themselves and in environments where they are rarely exposed to clashes of opinion. It is a weapon with which small-town bigots, conducting pogroms against Darwin, Marx, J. D. Salinger, Judy Blume, and other villains, seize control of school committees and library boards and terrorize teachers, librarians, and students.

Monoculturalists abuse history as flagrantly as multiculturalists. They sanitize the past and instill their own set of patriotic heroes and myths. This of course has happened before. I recently came upon a statement written by my father and adopted by the American Historical Association in 1941. "Genuine patriotism," the statement says,

> no less than honesty and sound scholarship, requires that textbook authors should endeavor to present a truthful picture of the past. Those who oppose this view would seem to believe that the history of the United States contains things so disgraceful that it is unsafe for the young to hear of them . . . To omit controversial question from the historical account, as is sometimes urged, would be to garble and distort the record. The history of the American people has been hammered out on the anvil of experience. It is a story of achievement, often against heavy odds. Some of the most glorious

passages have consisted in the struggle to overcome social and economic injustices.

The religious right is particularly well organized,
well funded, and ruthless. It plays a conspicuous role in
demanding the removal of heretical books from public
schools and libraries. It backs the movement to force
schools to place the Genesis doctrine of "creationism"
on the same scientific level as evolution. One conservative religious outfit, Citizens for Excellence in Education, recently unmasked Halloween as a pagan holiday
under cover of which witches pursue their wicked
schemes. The Reverend Pat Robertson has even resur-
rected the old theory that the ills of the modern world are
due to the diabolical work of Adam Weishaupt and the Il-
luminati in eighteenth-century Bavaria.

Remember Mr. Dooley's definition of a fanatic:
someone who "does what he thinks th' Lord would do if
He only knew th' facts in th' case." Honest, God-fearing,
unsophisticated persons who believe they are executing
the Lord's will are even a greater menace to the Bill of
Rights than self-important sophisticates on college campuses who at least do not see themselves as designated
batters for the Almighty.

Political correctness, whether of the left or the right,
is a blight on a free democracy. The First Amendment
has served the republic well. Whittling it down puts our
liberties at risk. As Tocqueville wrote a century and a half
ago, "It is by the enjoyment of a dangerous freedom that
Americans learn the art of rendering the dangers of freedom less formidable."

Appendix

☆ ☆ ☆ ☆

Schlesinger's Syllabus

The Baker's Dozen
Books Indispensable to an
Understanding of America

A dozen books? A hundred—or a thousand—books would not do the job. All countries are hard to understand, and, despite its brief history, the United States of America is harder to understand than most—because of its size in land and in people and because of its size in dreams, because of its braggadocio, because of its obstreperousness, and because of its heterogeneity. Still, for all this, the United States has an unmistakable national identity. Here, in chronological order, are a baker's dozen of books that have described, defined, and enriched America's sense of itself.

The Federalist (1787–1788) originated as an explanation and defense of the American Constitution. It survives as a brilliant exposition of the first principles of democratic government. Written mostly by Alexander Hamilton and James Madison, the eighty-five Federalist Papers were published between October 1787 and May 1788, in New York City newspapers, were reprinted throughout the thirteen states, and were read avidly during the debates over the ratification of the Constitution—and have been read avidly ever since. Can one imagine any newspaper today, even the august New York Times, running a series of such length and weight (except when blackmailed into doing so by the Unabomber)?

Thomas Jefferson, Writings (Library of America, 1984). Jefferson embodied much of American versatility within himself. He was an architect, an educator, an inventor, a paleontologist, an oenophile, a fiddler, an astute diplomat, a crafty politician, and a luminous prophet of liberty in words that light the human way through the centuries. President John F. Kennedy once called a dinner of Nobel Prize winners the most extraordinary collection of human knowledge ever to be gathered together at the White House "with the possible exception of when Thomas Jefferson dined alone."

But Jefferson was a man of contradictions: a champion of human freedom who did not, as George Washington had done, set his slaves free at his death; a champion of the free press who favored prosecuting ed-

itors for seditious libel; a champion of the strict construction of the Constitution who bent the sacred document for the sake of the Louisiana Purchase. Other early
presidents, observed Henry Adams, our most brilliant
historian, could be painted with broad brush strokes, but
Jefferson "could be painted only touch by touch, with a
fine pencil, and the perfection of the likeness depended
upon the shifting and uncertain flicker of its semi-
transparent shadows." That invaluable publishing project, the Library of America, brings together in a single
volume Jefferson's most notable writings including his
Autobiography, his major addresses, and a selection of
his letters.

Alexis de Tocqueville, *Democracy in America* (2 volumes, 1835, 1840). The concept of "national character"
has been under a cloud in scholarly circles, but can anyone really deny that Englishmen tend to be recognizably
different from Frenchmen, and Germans from Italians?
And can anyone read this extraordinary book about a
country of 13 million people along the Atlantic seaboard
without seeing how much of the description and analysis
still applies to the nation of 265 million stretching from
sea to sea?

When Tocqueville, a 25-year-old French nobleman,
arrived in the United States in 1831, he was more interested in democracy than he was in America—or rather
he was interested in America as a test case of the "great
democratic revolution" that, he felt, was "universal and
irresistible" and destined to transform the world. The
grand question was whether this revolution would lead to
"democratic liberty or democratic tyranny." Though con-

cerned about the "tyranny of the majority," Tocqueville believed that the power of voluntary associations and intermediate institutions had put America on the road to democratic liberty. He traveled around the country from May 1831 to February 1832 (and never came back). But in those nine months he saw more deeply into American institutions and the American character than anyone before or since. Over a century and a half later, his great work still illuminates American society.

Ralph Waldo Emerson, *Essays and Lectures* (Library of America, 1983). No one has expressed the American faith in the sovereignty of the individual more brilliantly, lyrically, and sardonically than Emerson. Born in 1803, trained for the Unitarian ministry, he left the pulpit for the lecture platform, from which he expounded his Transcendentalist philosophy in crackling aphorisms.

Some critics have decried what they regard as Emerson's shallow optimism, but underneath his alleged disregard of the problem of evil and his allegedly guileless faith in intuition lie shrewd, skeptical, hard-edged, almost ruthless Yankee insights into human nature. "For every benefit you receive," Emerson said, "a tax is levied." It is this tough side of Emerson that appealed in the nineteenth century to Hawthorne, Carlyle, and Nietzsche and that appeals to post-modernists today. The Library of America volume contains his masterly study of national character, *English Traits*, the penetrating biographical portraits in *Representative Men,* and his essays. For the tough-minded Emerson, read "History," "Self-reliance," and "Experience" and, in *The Conduct of Life,* "Power" and "Fate."

Harriet Beecher Stowe, *Uncle Tom's Cabin* (1852). She was forty years old, the wife of a professor of Biblical literature, the mother of seven children, when her indignation over the forced return of slaves to bondage under the Fugitive Slave Act led her to write the most influential novel in American history. The book sold 300,000 copies in its first year—equivalent to a sale of 3 million copies in the 1990s. Nine years after publication, the Civil War broke out. "So this is the little lady who made this big war," Lincoln is supposed to have said to her.

Uncle Tom's Cabin is remembered for its vivid depiction of the horrors of slavery—and often misremembered, because so many images derive from the stage versions rather than from the novel itself. *Uncle Tom's Cabin* is far more than the sentimental melodrama of "the Tom shows." It is a wonderfully shrewd and nuanced panorama of American life in the decade before the Civil War, rich in its variety of characters, settings, and perceptions. Mrs. Stowe may not in every respect meet contemporary standards of political correctness, but she was radical for her time in her insights and sympathies—one of the first, for example, to use the term "human rights." Frederick Douglass called *Uncle Tom's Cabin* a book "plainly marked by the finger of God."

Abraham Lincoln, *Speeches and Writings* (2 volumes, Library of America, 1989). The most miraculous of presidents, he was the best writer, the most intense moralist, with the most disciplined intelligence and the greatest strength of purpose—and yet he sprang out of the bleakest and most unpromising of circumstances. Confronting the supreme test and tragedy of American nationhood, he saw the crisis in perspective—"with malice toward none, with charity for all"—but never let perspective sever the nerve of action.

His Gettysburg Address amended the work of the Founding Fathers by leaving no doubt that the United States was a single nation based on the proposition that all men are created equal. And his Second Inaugural affirmed human limitations by declaring that "the Almighty has His own purposes"—purpose that erring mortals could never ascertain. "Men are not flattered," he later wrote, "by being shown that there has been a difference of purpose between the Almighty and them. To deny it, however, . . . is to deny that there is a God governing the world."

Mark Twain (Samuel Langhorne Clemens), *The Adventures of Huckleberry Finn* (1884). What piece of imaginative writing best expresses the spirit of America? A strong case can be made for Herman Melville's *Moby Dick,* for Walt Whitman's *Leaves of Grass,* for Nathaniel Hawthorne's *The Scarlet Letter.* But in the end one is compelled to go for *Huck Finn.*

This is because of the mordant way Mark Twain depicts antebellum America and the corruptions encouraged by a system in which people owned other people as private property—the hypocrisy, the sanctimoniousness, the humbuggery, the murderous feuds, the lynch mobs, the overhanging climate of brutality and violence.

It is also because of the language. *Huck Finn* is the first purely American novel. In it Mark Twain shows how the colloquial idiom spoken by an uneducated boy can express the most subtle perceptions and exquisite appreciations. The book liberated American writers. "All modern American literature," Ernest Hemingway wrote in *The Green Hills of Africa,* "comes from one book by Mark Twain called *Huckleberry Finn.* . . . All American writing comes from that. There was nothing before. There has been nothing so good since."

And it is because the novel's climactic scene so wonderfully dramatizes the essential American struggle of the individual against absolutes. Huck, responding for a moment to conventional morality, decides that the "plain hand of Providence" requires him to tell Miss Watson where she can locate Jim, her runaway slave and Huck's companion on the Mississippi raft. Huck feels suddenly virtuous, "all washed clean of sin for the first time I had ever felt so in my life." He reflects on his narrow escape: "how near I come to being lost and going to hell."

Then Huck begins to remember Jim and the rush of the great river and the singing and the laughing and the comradeship. He takes up the letter to Miss Watson, the letter of betrayal, and holds it in his hand. "I was a-trembling because I'd got to decide, forever, betwixt two things, and I knowed it. I studied a minute, sort of holding my breath, and then says to myself; 'All right, then, I'll go to hell'—and tore it up."

That, it may be said, is what America is all about. No wonder William Dean Howells called Mark Twain "the Lincoln of our literature."

James Bryce, *The American Commonwealth* (2 volumes, 1888). Bryce, a Scotsman born in Belfast in 1838, was one of those Victorian figures of fantastic energy, curiosity, versatility, and fluency, an expert in law, politics, diplomacy, history, literature, and mountaineering (Mount Bryce in the Rockies is named after him). He made his first visit to America in 1870 and, unlike Tocqueville, often came back, serving from 1907 to 1913 as British ambassador in Washington.

Bryce's mind was less probing and philosophical than Tocqueville's. His passion for facts had the ironic effect of making *The American Commonwealth* more dated than *Democracy in America,* since facts in America change all the time. But Bryce was a canny observer of institutions, and his observations have great value for historians. He spent much more time than Tocqueville on the party system and on state and local government. His chapters on "Why Great Men Are Not Chosen President" and "Why the Best Men Do Not Go into Politics" strike chords today. His analysis of the role of public opinion, "the great central point of the whole American polity," opened a new field of investigation. His aphorisms still reverberate: The Constitution "is the work of men who believed in original sin, and were resolved to leave open for transgressors no door which they could possibly shut." "The student of institutions, as well as the lawyer, is apt to overrate the effect of mechanical contrivances in politics." And, above all, "Perhaps no form of government needs great leaders so much as democracy."

William James, *Writings* (2 volumes, Library of America, 1992). The most American of philosophers, a wonderfully relaxed, humane, and engaging writer (his brother Henry, people used to say, wrote novels like a psychologist, while William wrote psychology like a novelist), he moved on from psychology to philosophy. James's pragmatism, with its argument that the meaning of ideas lies in their practical consequences, could not have been more in the American vein.

So too was his argument for pluralism and an open universe against those who contend for a monist system and a closed universe. People, James wrote, can discover partial and limited truths, truths that work for them, but no one can discover absolute truths. He rejected the notion that the world can be understood from a single point of view, as he rejected the assumption that all virtuous principles are in the end reconcilable and "the great single-word answers to the world's riddle" and "the pretence of finality in truth." He had an exhilarating faith in the adventure of an unfinished universe. The Library of America has done its usual masterful job in bringing his books and essays together in two compact volumes.

Henry Adams, *The Education of Henry Adams* (1918). Where William James saw the future as an exciting adventure, his friend and contemporary Henry

Adams looked on it with foreboding. Oppressed by the exponential rate of scientific and technological change, Adams doubted that the human mind could keep abreast of the relentless transformations wrought by the increasing velocity of history.

The challenge, as Adams saw it, was to control the new energies created and unleashed by science and technology. This required education, and looking back at his own education, Adams believed that "in essentials like religion, ethics, philosophy; in history, literature, art; in the concepts of all science, except perhaps mathematics, the American boy of 1854 [when he went to Harvard at the age of 16] stood nearer the year 1 than to the year 1900. The education he had received bore little relation to the education he needed."

The *Education* describes Adams's attempts to grapple with the emerging era. Along the way, he distributes fascinating portraits of politicians and writers, fascinating accounts of historical episodes, fascinating reflections on the changing world: "The new Americans," he said, "must, whether they were fit or unfit, create a world of their own, a science, a society, a philosophy, a universe, where they had not yet created a road or even learned to dig their own iron." Could the new Americans rise to the challenge?

"Man has mounted science and is now run away with," he had written in 1862, when the *Monitor* and the *Merrimac* were foreshadowing new technologies in the instrumentation of war. "I firmly believe that before many centuries more, science will be the master of man. The engines he will have invented will be beyond his strength to control. Some day science shall have the existence of mankind in its power, and the human race commit suicide by blowing up the world."

H. L. Mencken, *The American Language* (1936; supplements, 1945, 1948). Mencken, of course (but why do I write "of course"?—he is very likely a forgotten man today), was one of the literary heroes of the 1920s. He was a master of exuberant irreverence, and he presented his satirical take on America with swashbuckling vigor of style and a liberating polemical tone. But in the 1930s Mencken fell out of sync with the national mood. The great cultural heretic of the twenties, he was a libertarian, not a democrat, and, suddenly confronted by the harsh political antagonisms of the thirties, he seemed sour and mean-spirited.

But to his fans he redeemed himself by *The American Language,* his shrewd, copious, quite scholarly, highly entertaining account of the way a new language has evolved out of the English spoken across the sea. This rich and readable book is a wonderful compendium of Americana. It shows, among other things, that assimilation, far from an unconditional surrender to Anglocentrism, has been a two-way street in which non-Anglo newcomers play an active part in transforming the English into the American language.

Gunnar Myrdal, *An American Dilemma* (1944). Racism has been an organic element in American life from the start. Jefferson had mixed views on the subject of race; Tocqueville had prescient comments along with mistaken prophecies; Mark Twain was haunted by the enigma of race; for Lincoln it was a central issue. But most of the time the race question has been ignored or denied. It took a Swedish economist commissioned by an American foundation to undertake the first full-dress, comprehensive study of black-white relations. Heading a team that included such black scholars as Ralph Bunche and Kenneth B. Clark, Gunnar Myrdal produced *An American Dilemma* in 1944, eighty-one years after Lincoln's Emancipation Proclamation.

This powerful work was not only an analysis: it was a challenge. Written during the war against Hitler and his theory of a master race, it called on Americans to discard their own theories of racial superiority and live up to the promises of equality implicit in what Myrdal termed the American Creed. Myrdal was unduly optimistic in thinking that the American Creed by itself could overcome the pathologies of racism. But his work encouraged the activism of blacks, and it pricked the consciences of whites. And the account it offers of the conditions under which black Americans lived, worked, and died half a century ago provide a heartening measure of the changes that have taken place since the publication of *An American Dilemma*.

Reinhold Niebuhr, *The Irony of American History* (1952). The most influential American theologian of the century, Niebuhr approached American history from a neo-orthodox religious perspective—that is, from a tempered, non-fundamentalist belief in original sin (defined as the self-pride that mistakes the relative for the absolute), in the ambiguities of human nature, in divine judgment on human pretensions, and in the incompleteness of life within history. It is necessary, he wrote in this book, to understand "the limits of all human striving, the fragmentariness of all human wisdom, the precariousness of all historic configurations of power, and the mixture of good and evil in all human virtue."

Like William James, Niebuhr was a relativist and a pluralist who scorned monists and absolutists. Like Lincoln, he was especially critical of those whose vainglory leads them to suppose they grasp the purposes of the Almighty. By irony Niebuhr meant the situation that arises when the consequences of an action are contrary to the intentions of the actors because of weaknesses inherent in the actors themselves. This concept informed his reading of American history. Americans, Niebuhr felt, are too much inclined to believe in their own innocence and righteousness and too reluctant to recognize the self-regard in their own souls. He deplored the national inability "to comprehend the depth of evil to which individuals and communities may sink, particularly when they try to play the role of God to history."

Niebuhr's interpretation of the American past is wise and chastening, and it is deep in the American tradition. His conception of democracy is akin to that of the men who made the Constitution. "Man's capacity for justice makes democracy possible," he wrote in *The Children of Light and the Children of Darkness*; "but man's inclination to injustice makes democracy necessary."

Notes on
Sources

☆ ☆ ☆ ☆

FOREWORD

The quotation on p. 13 is from John Stuart Mill, *Representative Government,* chap. xvi.

The quotation on p. 14 is from "War in Europe," *Economist,* July 6, 1991.

The quotation on p. 14 is from John Grimond, "For Want of Glue," *Economist,* June 29, 1991.

The Michael Ignatieff quotation on p. 14 is from "A Rich Nation Is Tearing Itself Apart," London *Observer,* June 9, 1991.

The Chinua Achebe quotation on p. 15 is from "The High Price of Patience," *New York Times,* July 27, 1993.

The quotations on pp. 15–16 are from Letter III in Crèvecoeur's *Letters from an American Farmer* (1782). Emphasis added in the last sentence.

The George Bancroft quotation on pp. 16–17 is from *Literary and Historical Miscellanies* (New York, 1855), p. 508.

Sir John Macdonald's remark on p. 17 is from "For Want of Glue," *Economist,* June 29, 1991.

The Tocqueville quotation on p. 19 is from James T. Schleifer, *The Making of Tocqueville's Democracy in America* (Chapel Hill, 1980), p. 66.

Woodrow Wilson's quotation on pp. 21–22 is from Wilson, *The New Freedom* (New York, 1913), p. 68.

The quotation from Mario Cuomo on p. 23 is from his statement of July 15, 1991, on multicultural education.

The Fitzgerald quotation on p. 24 is from *The Crack-Up.*

The Gandhi quotation on pp. 24–25 is from E. W. Desmond, "Storm Over India," *New York Review of Books,* May 14, 1992.

CHAPTER 1

The first quotation on p. 29 is from Thomas Paine's *Common Sense,* appendix; the second is from Herman Melville's *White Jacket,* chap. 36.

The quotations on pp. 29–30 are from Melville's *Redburn,* chap. 33; *Emerson in His Journals,* ed. Joel Porte (Cambridge, 1982), p. 347; and George Washington's *Writings,* ed. J. C. Fitzpatrick (Washington, 1938), xxvii, 252; xxxiv, 23. Emphasis added.

John Quincy Adams's quotation on p. 31 is from a letter written by Adams to Baron von Furstenwaerther and published in Werner Sollors' book *Beyond Ethnicity* (New York, 1986), p. 4. Emphasis added.

Alexis de Tocqueville's quotation on p. 31 is from a letter written by Tocqueville to Ernest de Chabrol dated June 9, 1831, and published in Tocqueville's *Selected Letters on Politics and Society,* ed. Roger Boesche (Berkeley, 1985), p. 38.

Tocqueville's quotation on pp. 31–32 is from his book *Democracy in America*, vol. I (1835), chap. xiv.

The Lincoln quotation on p. 32 is from his speech in Chicago, July 10, 1858, Abraham Lincoln, *Speeches and Writings, 1832–1858* (Library of America), pp. 455–456.

James Bryce's quotation on p. 33 is from his book *The American Commonwealth*, vol. II (London, 1888), pp. 709, 328.

Gunnar Myrdal's quotation on p. 33 is from his book *An American Dilemma* (1944; 20th-anniversary edition, New York, 1962), chap. 1.

Herman Melville's quotation on p. 34 is from his book *Redburn*, chap. 33.

W. E. B. Du Bois's quotation on p. 35 is from his book *Dusk of Dawn* (Harcourt, Brace & Co., 1940). Also published in *Writings* (New American Library), p. 563.

Abraham Lincoln's quotation on p. 36 is from a letter written by Lincoln to Joshua F. Speed dated August 24, 1855, and published in Lincoln's *Speeches and Writings, 1832–1858*, p. 363.

Frederick Jackson Turner's quotation on p. 36 is from his book *The Frontier in American History* (New York, 1920), pp. 22–23.

James Bryce's quotation on p. 36 is from *The American Commonwealth*, vol. II, p. 329.

Henry James's quotations on pp. 37–38 are from his book *The American Scene* (1906; Horizon Press edition, 1967) pp. 64, 120–21, 132, 139.

The Melting-Pot and Jane Addams's quotation on pp. 38–39 are from Arthur Mann's book *The One and the Many* (Chicago, 1979), pp. 98–100, 110, 192; and Milton Gordon's book *Assimilation in American Life* (New York, 1964), pp. 120–21.

The quotation from a Jewish reviewer on p. 40 is from Arthur Mann's *The One and the Many*, p. 113.

Woodrow Wilson's quotation on p. 41 is from his address to foreign-born citizens on May 10, 1915, in Philadelphia, which was published in Wilson's *The Messages and Papers of Woodrow Wilson*, ed. Albert Shaw (New York, 1924), vol. I, pp. 115–16.

Theodore Roosevelt's quotation on p. 41 is from his address in New York on September 10, 1917, and published in his *Works* (Memorial edition), chap. XXI, p. 38; also from the April 16, 1918, editorial in the *Kansas City Star;* and from the book *Roosevelt in the Kansas City Star,* ed. Ralph Stout (Boston, 1921), p. 137.

Horace Kallen's quotations on p. 42 are from the February 18 and 25, 1915, issues of *The Nation* and from his book *Culture and Democracy in the United States* (New York, 1924), pp. 116, 122, 124.

Nicholas Roosevelt's quotation on p. 42 is from *The New York Times* and Arthur Mann's *The One and the Many*, p. 142.

Franklin D. Roosevelt's quotation on p. 43 is from a letter to Henry L. Stimson dated February 1, 1943. The occasion, ironically, was the formation of a combat team of American citizens of Japanese ancestry. The first sentence quoted was written by Elmer Davis, distinguished journalist and head of the Office of War Information; see Bill Hosokawa's *Nisei: The Quiet Americans* (New York, 1969), pp. 365–66.

Alexis de Tocqueville's quotation on p. 44 is from his book *Democracy in America*, vol. I, chap. xviii.

Gunnar Myrdal's quotation on p. 45 is from *An American Dilemma*, pp. 4, 13, 809, 880.

The Michael Novak quotation on p. 47 is from *The Rise of the Unmeltable Ethnics* (New York, 1972), p. 270.

Marcus Lee Hansen's quotation on p. 47 is from his article "The Problem of the Third Generation Immigrant," reprinted and introduced by Oscar Handlin in the November 1952 edition of *Commentary*. The second generation, according to Hansen, tended to be "traitors" who in their passion to be accepted as Americans worked overtime to divest themselves of their past—the past that the third generation, more securely American, then seeks to recover. Hansen's Law can be pushed too far. As Werner Sollors points out, Hansen himself, Oscar Handlin (the historian who did much to popularize Hansen's Law), and my father (who long advocated the writing of immigration history and, after Hansen's premature death, put his last two books in shape for publication) were all second-generation sons of foreign-born fathers; see Sollors' *Beyond Ethnicity*, p. 218.

Gunnar Myrdal's quotation on p. 48 is from "The Case Against Romantic Ethnicity," Dialogue Discussion Paper, Center for the Study of Democratic Institutions, May 13, 1974, pp. 9, 17.

The quotation "the unmeltable ethnics" on p. 49 is from Michael Novak's *The Rise of the Unmeltable Ethnics* (New York, 1972).

The passage concerning the Ethnic Heritage Studies Act on p. 49 is based on Arthur Mann's *The One and the Many*, pp. 167–68.

CHAPTER 2

The quotation on p. 52 is from George Orwell's *1984* (New York, 1949), p. 251.

Ernest Gellner's quotation on p. 53 is from his book *Thought and Change* (London, 1964), p. 168.

J. H. Plumb's quotation on p. 54 is from his book *The Death of the Past* (Boston, 1969), p. 40.

Isaiah Berlin's quotation on pp. 54–55 is from his book *The Crooked Timber of Humanity* (London, 1990), pp. 246–47.

Eric Foner's quotation on p. 56 is from his article "Restructuring Yesterday's News," *Harper's,* December 1990, p. 70.

Saburō Ienaga's quotation on p. 56 is from his book *The Pacific War: World War II and the Japanese, 1931–1945* (New York, 1978), p. xi; see also Steven R. Weisman's article "Japan and the War: Debate on Censors is Renewed," *The New York Times,* October 8, 1989.

Michael Stürmer's quotation on p. 57 is from Richard J. Evans's *In Hitler's Shadow* (New York, 1989), pp. 19, 103, 179.

Milan Kundera's quotation on pp. 57–58 is from his book *The Book of Laughter and Forgetting* (1979; Penguin edition, 1981), pp. 3, 159.

Vaclav Havel's quotation on p. 58 is from Henry Kamm's article "Two Heads of State Call on Waldheim," *The New York Times,* July 27, 1990.

The quotation from Arthur Schlesinger, Jr.'s grandfather on p. 58 is from the introduction to Arthur M. Schlesinger, Sr.'s *The Birth of the Nation* (New York, 1968), p. v.

Andrew Hacker's quotation on p. 59 is from his article "Do Schools Teach Bias to Kids?," *New York Newsday,* September 10, 1989.

William Hale Thompson's quotations on p. 60 are from Arthur M. Schlesinger, Sr.'s book *In Retrospect: The History of a Historian* (New York, 1963), pp. 103–5.

John V. Kelleher's quotation on p. 61 is from his article "A Long Way From Tipperary," *Reporter,* May 12, 1960.

Peggy Noonan's quotation on p. 62 is from her article "What New Americans Need to Know," *The Wall Street Journal,* November 21, 1990.

Allan Bloom's quotation on p. 62 is from his book *The Closing of the American Mind* (New York, 1987), pp. 29, 56.

Pieter Geyl's quotation on p. 63 is from his book *Napoleon For and Against* (1949; Peregrine paperback, 1965), p. 18.

Frederick Jackson Turner's quotation on p. 64 is from his book *The Frontier in American History*, p. 24.

W. E. B. Du Bois's quotation on p. 64 is from his book *Black Reconstruction* (New York, 1935), pp. 725, 727.

President Kennedy's quotation on p. 64 is from Arthur M. Schlesinger, Jr.'s book *A Thousand Days* (Boston, 1965), p. 966.

Herbert Aptheker's quotation on p. 65 is from the introduction to *William Styron's Nat Turner: Ten Black Writers Respond,* ed. John Henrik Clarke (New York, 1968), p. vii.

Malcolm X's quotation on p. 65 is from a leaflet advertising the Second National Conference, "The Infusion of African & African American Content in the School Curriculum," Atlanta, Georgia, November 1–4, 1990.

In regard to black psychologists' arguments on p. 65, see, for example, Edmund W. Gordon, Fayneese Miller, and David Rollock's article "Coping with Communicentric Bias in Knowledge Production in the Social Sciences," *Educational Researcher,* April 1990. Black scholars are no more immune than white scholars to the temptations of pretentious jargon.

Maulana Karenga's quotation on pp. 65–66 is from his book *Introduction to Black Studies* (Los Angeles, 1982), pp. 42, 43. Asante's comment is on the back cover.

The quotation on p. 66 is from Larry Cuban's article "Black History and White Folk," *Saturday Review,* September 21, 1968.

Melville J. Herskovits' quotation on p. 66 is from his book *The Myth of the Negro Past* (New York, 1941), p. 299.

Jacob Gordon's quotation on p. 67 is from Isabel Wilkerson's article "Facing Grim Data on Young Males, Blacks Grope for Ways to End Blight," *The New York Times,* July 17, 1990.

Felix Boateng's quotation on p. 67 is from the book *Going to School: The African-American Experience,* ed. Kofi Lomotey (Albany, 1990), pp. 14, 73, 79.

Maulana Karenga's quotation on p. 67 is from *Introduction to Black Studies,* pp. 25–27.

Molefi Kete Asante's quotation on p. 67 is from Debra Viadero's article "Battle Over Multicultural Education Rises in Intensity," *Education Week,* November 28, 1990, p. 11. His quotation on p. 68 is from Carol Innerst's article "Putting Africa on the Map," *The Washington Times,* November 13, 1990.

Clare Jacob's quotation on p. 68 is from Jane Caulton's article "D.C. Joins Other School Systems in Push for Afrocentric Reforms," *The Washington Times,* August 6, 1990.

Charles Willie's quotation on p. 68 is from Glenn M. Rickett's article "Multiculturalism Mobilizes," *Academic Questions,* Summer 1990, p. 64.

The quotation on p. 68 attributed to a scholar is from I. A. Newby's article "Historians and Negroes," *Journal of Negro History,* January 1969, p. 33.

Asa Hilliard's quotation on p. 68 is from Anthony DePalma's article "The Culture Question," *The New York Times,* supplement on education, November 4, 1990.

Na'im Akbar's quotation on pp. 68–69 is from Joyce Braden Harris's *African and African-American Traditions in Language Arts* (Portland Baseline Essay), p. 30.

The quotations on p. 69 regarding the Ebonics controversy are from Louis Menand, "Johnny Be Good," *The New Yorker,* January 13, 1997; Reuben Abati, *The Baltimore Sun,* January 23, 1997; Sharpton in *The New York Post,* December 23, 1996.

Amos Wilson's quotation on p. 70 is from Maulana Karenga's *Introduction to Black Studies,* pp. 338–40.

Molefi Kete Asante's quotations on pp. 70–71 are from his book *Afrocentricity* (revised edition, Trenton, 1988), pp. 1, 2, 20, 38, 43, 67.

Leonard Jeffries's quotation on p. 73 is from Joseph Berger's article "Professors' Theories on Race Stir Turmoil at City College," *The New York Times,* April 20, 1990; Tim Spofford's article "State's Schools Smother Black Culture, Professor Says," *The Times Union,* Albany, New York, March 22, 1990; and Carol Innerst's article "Putting Africa on the Map."

The quotations about the new curriculum on pp. 73–74 are from "A Curriculum of Inclusion, Report of the Commissioner's Task Force on Minorities: Equity and Excellence," July 1989, pp. iii, iv, 1, 16, 21, 34, 35, and from the appendix, pp. 9, 24, 25. The commentator who objected to "slaves" is Cybele Raver of the Yale Department of Psychology in a memorandum to Ed Lalor of the New York State Department of Education, December 17, 1990.

Asa Hilliard's quotation on p. 74 is from his article "Free Your

Mind, Return to the Source: The African Origin of Civilization"
(mimeograph), pp. 6, 12, 19, 21, 23.

John Henrik Clarke's quotation on p. 75 is from *Social Studies
African-American Baseline Essay* (Portland, 1987), pp. 4, 8–11,
56, 60.

The quotation on p. 76 concerning other Baseline Essays' arguments is from Michael D. Harris's book *African-American Art Traditions and Developments* (Portland, 1987), p. 2.

Leonard Jeffries's quotation on p. 76 is from Tim Spofford's article "State's Schools Smother Black Culture."

The passage concerning Napoleon on p. 76 is from Carol Innerst's article "Multiethnic Education Aims for History's Untold Stories," *The Washington Times,* November 13, 1990.

Edward W. Said's quotation on p. 77 is from his article "Ignorant
Armies Clash by Night," *The Nation,* February 11, 1991.

CHAPTER 3

The quotation on p. 80 is from Roger Kimball's article "The Pe-
riphery vs. the Center: The MLA in Chicago," *The New Criterion,*
February 1991, p. 17.

Arthur Schlesinger, Jr.'s quotation on p. 81 is from his article
"Nationalism and History," *Journal of Negro History,* January 1969,
p. 19.

Frank M. Snowden, Jr.'s quotation on p. 82 is from his article
"Bernal's 'Blacks,' Herodotus, and Other Classical Evidence,"
Arethusa, Fall 1989, pp. 83, 84.

Frank J. Yurco's first quotation on p. 83 is from his article "Were
the Ancient Egyptians Black or White?," *Biblical Archeology Review,*
September–October 1989. His second quotation is from a letter he
wrote to Erich Martel dated November 14, 1990. Mr. Martel has
done yeoman work in trying to persuade the Washington school system of the sham scholarship involved in the Afrocentric curriculum.

Mary Lefkowitz's book mentioned on p. 83 is *Not Out of Africa:
How Afrocentrism Became an Excuse to Teach Myth as History* (New
York, 1996). Appiah's comment is on the jacket. See also Mary
Lefkowitz and G. M. Rogers, eds., *Black Athena Revisited* (Chapel
Hill, 1996).

Carter Woodson's quotation on p. 84 is from his book *The Negro in Our History* (Washington, 1922), p. 10.

The passage from L. Pearce Williams on p. 84 is from his letter "Did Egypt Originate Geometry Theorem?," *The New York Times,* February 14, 1991.

Diane Ravitch's quotation on p. 84 is from her article "Multiculturalism," *American Scholar,* Summer 1990, p. 347.

The Drew quotation on p. 85 is from H. H. Adams III's essay "African and African-American Contributions to Science and Technology" (Portland, 1987), p. 77. For the correction (and a multitude of other facts and insights) I am indebted to Diane Ravitch. Spencie Love's quotation is from her book *One Blood: The Death and Resurrection of Charles R. Drew* (Chapel Hill, 1996), p. 4.

Bill Graves is the reporter quoted on p. 85. His quotation comes from his article "Africanized History Opens Eyes," *Portland Oregonian,* November 18, 1990.

Wade Nobles's quotation on p. 87 is from Maulana Karenga's *Introduction to Black Studies.*

Léopold Senghor's quotation on p. 87 is from Roger Shattuck and Samba Ka's article "Born Again African," *The New York Review of Books,* December 20, 1990.

David Walker's quotation on pp. 87–88 is from Lawrence H. Fuchs's book *The American Kaleidoscope* (Hanover, 1990), p. 151.

Frederick Douglass's quotation on p. 88 is from his article "African Civilization Society," in *Douglass' Monthly,* February 1859, reprinted in Philip S. Foner, ed., *Life and Writings of Frederick Douglass* (New York, 1950), II, 443.

The quotation on p. 88 is from David Gerber's *Black Ohio and the Color Line, 1860–1915* (Urbana, 1976), p. 182; quoted by Judith Stein in *The Invention of Ethnicity,* edited by Werner Sollors (New York, 1989), p. 81.

W. E. B. Du Bois's quotation on p. 88 is from *Dusk of Dawn,* p. 116, and from *Writings* (Library of America), pp. 639, 755; see also *W. E. B. Du Bois: A Reader,* ed. Meyer Weinberg (New York, 1970), p. 373; and Orlando Patterson's article "Rethinking Black History," *Harvard Educational Review,* August 1971, p. 310. Emphasis added.

Abram L. Harris's quotation on p. 89 is from his book *Race, Radicalism, and Reform,* and from J. S. Butler's article "Multiple Identities," *Society,* May–June 1990, p. 9.

Horace Mann Bond's quotation on p. 89 is from *The New York Times,* June 27, 1959; see also Milton Gordon's book *Assimilation in American Life,* pp. 15, 113.

Martin Luther King Jr.'s quotation on p. 89 is from Robert Penn Warren's book *Who Speaks for the Negro?* (New York, 1965), p. 216.

The passage concerning Alex Haley on p. 90 is from Werner Sollors' *The Invention of Ethnicity,* p. 227.

LeRoi Jones's quotation on p. 90 is from his book *Home* (New York, 1966), p. 111.

The passage on p. 91 concerning Arthur Smith is from Molefi Kete Asante's book *Afrocentricity,* p. 29; see also William Raspberry's article "Euro, Afro and Other Eccentric 'Centrics,' " *The Washington Post,* September 10, 1990.

Wade Nobles's quotation on pp. 91–92 is from accounts by Andrew Sullivan in his article "Racism 101," *The New Republic,* November 26, 1990, and by Carol Innerst in her article, "Multiethnic Education Aims for History's Untold Stories," *The Washington Post,* November 13, 1990.

Nathan Huggins's quotation on p. 92 is from his article in *Center Magazine,* July–August 1974; see also Werner Sollors' *Beyond Ethnicity,* pp. 13, 14.

The passage on p. 92 concerning Professor Asante is from his April 6, 1989, lecture at Rider College, cited in A. F. Scrupski's article "Multiculturalism: Political Wolf Under Educational Sheepskin," *Measure,* February–March 1990, p. 4.

William Raspberry's quotation on p. 92 is from his article "Euro, Afro and Other Eccentric 'Centrics.' "

The David Riesman quotation on p. 93 is from Jonathan Zimmerman, "Beyond Double Consciousness: Black Peace Corps Volunteers in Africa, 1961–1971," *Journal of American History,* December 1995, p. 1001.

Henry Adams's quotation on p. 93 is from *Education,* chap. xvi.

The quotation on p. 94 is from the California Task Force report *Toward a State of Self-Esteem* (1960), p. 4.

The quotation on p. 95 from the New York report can be found in "One Nation, Many Peoples: A Declaration of Cultural Interdependence," Report of the New York State Social Studies Review and Development Committee, June 1991.

The Rodriguez quotation on p. 95 is from Richard Rodriguez, *Days of Obligation* (New York, 1992), 169.

Frederick Douglass's quotation on p. 96 is from his book *Narrative of the Life of . . . an American Slave* (1845; Anchor paperback, 1989), pp. 42, 43, and his book *My Bondage and My Freedom* (New York, 1855), pp. 156–58.

W. E. B. Du Bois's quotation on p. 97 is from his book *The Souls of Black Folk;* see also *Writings* (Library of America), p. 438.

Ralph Ellison's first quotation on p. 97 is from Jim Sleeper's book *The Closest of Strangers* (New York, 1990), p. 234; his later quotation was from *The New Republic,* December 24, 1990.

Sterling A. Brown, Arthur P. Davis, and Ulysses Lee's quotation on p. 97 are from the book they edited, *The Negro Caravan: Writings by American Negroes* (New York, 1941), pp. 6, 7.

William Raspberry's quotation on p. 99 is from his article "Euro, Afro and Other Eccentric 'Centrics.' "

Jacques Barzun's quotation on p. 99 is from a letter from Barzun to Diane Ravitch dated February 26, 1991.

A. A. Schomburg's quotation on p. 100 is from Benjamin Quarles's article "What the Historian Owes the Negro," *Saturday Review,* September 3, 1966.

Orlando Patterson's quotation on p. 100 is from his article "Rethinking Black History," p. 305.

John Hope Franklin's quotation on p. 100 is from his book *Race and History* (Baton Rouge, 1989), p. ix.

Asa Hilliard's quotation on pp. 100–101 is from Bill Graves's article "Africanized History Opens Eyes."

Don Smith, chairman of the education department at City University of New York's Baruch College, is the author defending the New York task-force report quoted on p. 101. He is also quoted in Katti Gray's article "Black Group Rallying for Curriculum," *Newsday,* July 22, 1990.

Diane Ravitch's quotations on pp. 101–2 are from her article "History and the Perils of Pride" (manuscript); see also Debra Viadero's articles "History Curricula Stir Controversy in Largest State," *Education Week,* August 1, 1990, and "Battle Over Multicultural Education Rises in Intensity," *Education Week,* November 28, 1990; and Dexter Waugh's article "California Minorities Fight 'Chauvinistic' School Books," *Washington Times,* January 30, 1991.

The passage concerning the Iroquois lobby on p. 102 is from Diane Ravitch's article "Multiculturalism," *American Scholar,* Summer 1990, pp. 346, 347; William A. Starna's letter "Whose History Will

Be Taught?," *The New York Times*, March 7, 1990; and Mark Oppenheimer, "Tribal Lore," *Lingua Franca*, March 1997. The Irish Famine bill is Assembly Bill No. 6510, amending the state education law.

Alan L. Benosky is the retired state history teacher quoted on p. 103 from his letter to *Newsday*, July 15, 1990.

The quotation on p. 103 is from the Department of History at the State University of New York and a letter from Kenneth P. O'Brien, the chair of the SUNY Brockport history department, to CUNY Graduate School, dated November 25, 1990.

Franklyn Jenifer's quotation on pp. 103–4 is from Jacob Weisburg's interview with Jenifer, "Franklyn Jenifer: Taking Howard University Into Slum Neighborhoods," *The Los Angeles Times*, February 10, 1991.

Gore Vidal's quotation on p. 104 is from Jon Wiener's article "The Scholar Squirrels and the National Security State: An Interview with Gore Vidal," *Radical History Review*, Spring 1989, p. 136.

CHAPTER 4

William Raspberry's quotation on p. 106 is from his article "Euro, Afro and Other Eccentric 'Centrics.' "

Chief Justice Warren's quotation on p. 107 is from *Brown* v. *Board of Education of Topeka*, 347 U.S. 483 (1954).

The quotations from Felix Boateng and Janice Hale-Benson on p. 107 are from *Going to School: The African-American Experience*, ed. Kofi Lomotey, pp. 82, 216.

Alan Kors is the University of Pennsylvania professor quoted on p. 108. His quotation is from Mona Charen's article "A Losing Battle v. Campus Thought Police," *Newsday*, December 5, 1990.

The Brown University quotation on p. 108 is from Mary Jordan, "Colleges Rethink Voluntary Segregation," *International Herald Tribune*, March 8, 1994.

Jacob Weisberg's quotation on p. 108 is from his article "Thin Skins," *The New Republic*, February 18, 1991.

The quotation on p. 108 from a black student at Central Michigan University is from the *Chronicle of Higher Education*, quoted in Dinesh D'Souza's article "The New Segregation on Campus," *American Scholar*, Winter 1991, p. 19.

Signithia Fordham's quotation on pp. 108–9 is from Seth My-
dans's article "Black Identity vs. Success and Seeming 'White,' " *The
New York Times,* April 25, 1990.

The quotation concerning the University of California at Berkeley's Budget Committee on p. 109 is from Stephen R. Barnett's article "Get Back," *The New Republic,* February 18, 1991.

Henry Louis Gates's quotation on p. 109 is from *The Detroit
News,* January 31, 1991.

John Hope Franklin's quotation on p. 109 is from his book *Race
and History,* p. 301.

The quotation concerning Jonathan Pryce on p. 109 is from
Mervyn Rothstein's article "Union Bars White in Asian Role," *The
New York Times,* August 8, 1990; Joseph C. Koenenn's article "Efforts
at Casting Compromise," *Newsday,* August 10, 1990. Actors' Equity
later rescinded the ban against Pryce.

Shirley MacLaine's quotation on p. 110 is from Arthur
Schlesinger, Jr., "Same Difference," *American Theatre,* April 1993.

August Wilson's quotation on p. 110 is from his article " 'I Want
a Black Director,' " *The New York Times,* September 26, 1990.

Kenneth B. Clark's quotation on pp. 111–12 is from his "Letter
of Resignation From Board of Directors of Antioch College," *Black
Studies: Myths & Realities,* introduced by Bayard Rustin (New York,
1969), p. 32.

In regard to the passage about printing federal laws in German
on p. 112, see the clarifying letter by Dennis Baron in the *Times Literary Supplement,* September 1–7, 1989.

Alfredo Mathew, Jr.'s quotation on p. 113 is from Rosalie Pedalino Porter's book *Forked Tongue* (New York, 1990), p. 7.

Richard Rodriguez's first quotation on pp. 113–14 is from his article "Unilingual, Not Unilateral," *The Wall Street Journal,* June 25,
1985. His second quotation is from his book *Hunger of Memory*
(Boston, 1982), pp. 19, 27.

Mario Cuomo's quotation on p. 114 is from William E. Leucht-
enburg's article "Most Americans Don't Know What Lincoln Really
Represents," *American Heritage,* December 1990, pp. 59, 60.

Rosalie Pedalino Porter's quotation on p. 114 is from her book
Forked Tongue, pp. 217, 218. See also two other articles: "Bilingual
Education Has Muted the Future for Minority Children," *Washing-
ton Post National Weekly,* April 30–May 6, 1990, and "The Case for
English Immersion," *Teacher Magazine,* August 1990.

The congressman who invoked Shakespeare against the amendment on p. 115 was Frank Pallone, Jr., of New Jersey, *Congressional Record,* August 1, 1996, p. H9755.

The Niebuhr quotation on p. 116 is from Reinhold Niebuhr, *Man's Nature and His Communities* (New York, 1965), p. 84.

Edward Koch's quotation on p. 117 is from Koch "When Prominent Blacks Engage in Overt Racism," *New York Post,* August 16, 1991.

The quotations from Leonard Jeffries and William Raspberry on p. 117 are from Jason DeParle's article "Talk of Government Being Out to Get Blacks Falls on More Attentive Ears," *The New York Times,* October 29, 1990.

Richard Rodriguez's quotation on p. 118 is from his article "Unilingual, Not Unilateral."

The passage on p. 119 concerning posters at the University of Michigan is from Dinesh D'Souza's article "Illiberal Education," *The Atlantic,* March 1991, p. 52.

Justice Oliver Wendell Holmes's quotation on p. 119 is from *United States v. Schwimmer,* 279 U.S. 644 (1928).

For more information about the debate over the First Amendment on p. 119, see the interesting, though (for me) ultimately unconvincing, argument in Mary Ellen Gale's article "On Curbing Racial Speech," *The Responsive Community,* Winter 1990–91, pp. 47–61.

The passage concerning the American Civil Liberties Union on pp. 119–20 is from Anthony DePalma's article "Battling Bias, Campuses Face Free Speech Fight," *The New York Times,* February 20, 1991.

Kenneth B. Clark's quotation on p. 120 is from his "Letter of Resignation," p. 33.

Dinesh D'Souza's comment on p. 120 is from his article "The New Segregation," *American Scholar,* Winter 1995, p. 21.

The bulletin from the Office of Student Affairs at Smith College on pp. 120–21 is from John Taylor's article "Are You Politically Correct?," *New York,* January 21, 1991.

The philosopher's quotation on p. 121 is from Mona Charen's article "A Losing Battle."

The quotations concerning Bernard Bailyn and Stephan Thernstrom on pp. 121–22 are from a letter from Paula Ford and Penelope Codrington to Stephan Thernstrom dated March 9, 1988.

The quotations on pp. 122–23 concerning correspondence between a University of Pennsylvania student and an administrator are from A. C. Kors's article "It's Speech, Not Sex, the Dean Bans Now," *The Wall Street Journal,* October 12, 1989.

Theodore Roosevelt's quotation on p. 124 is from his *Works* (Memorial edition, New York, 1923–26) chap. XX, p. 456.

CHAPTER 5

Stephan Thernstrom's quotation on p. 127 is from his article "The Minority Majority Will Never Come," *The Wall Street Journal,* July 26, 1990.

For a historian's cogent discussion about the last paragraph, p. 127, see Otis Graham, Jr.'s article "Immigration and the National Interest" in *U.S. Immigration in the 1980s: Reappraisal and Reform,* ed. David Simcox (Westview Press, 1988), pp. 124–36.

The quotation on p. 128 is from Nathan Newman to the editors of *Dissent,* Summer 1989, p. 413.

The quotation on p. 129 concerning European classical music is from Clyde Moneyhun's letter "Culture Schlock," *The New Republic,* March 4, 1991; see also Edward Rothstein's article "Roll Over Beethoven," *The New Republic,* February 4, 1991.

The passage citing the National Endowment for the Humanities on p. 129 is from Lynne V. Cheney's book *Fifty Hours: A Core Curriculum for College Students* (Washington, 1989), p. 7.

The passage on p. 129 concerning required courses in third-world or ethnic studies is from Dinesh D'Souza's "Illiberal Education," p. 53.

Pearce Williams's quotation on p. 130 is from his article "Did Egypt Originate Geometry Theorem?"

Henry A. Giroux is the first professor quoted on p. 131. His quotation is from John Searle's article "The Storm Over the University," *The New York Review of Books,* December 6, 1990.

Stanley Hauerwas of the Duke Divinity School is the second professor quoted on p. 131. His quotation is from Pam Kelley's article "For Duke Profs, The Hot Debate Is What to Teach," *The Charlotte Observer,* September 28, 1990. I have supplied the full word that the *Observer* primly rendered as "—holes."

The passage about Marxists on p. 131 is from Irving Howe's admirable essay "The Value of the Canon," *The New Republic,* February 18, 1991.

The Richburg quotations on p. 134 are from his article "A Black American in Africa," *Washington Post National Weekly Edition,* April 10–16, 1995, and his book *Out of America: A Black Man Confronts Africa* (New York, 1997).

The passage on p. 134 concerning Algerian women is from Frantz Fanon's book *A Dying Colonialism* (London, 1965), pp. 37, 46.

Margaret Thatcher's quotation on p. 135 is from David S. Broder's article "Her View of the U.S. Had a Euro-Cynical Bent," *International Herald Tribune,* March 13, 1991.

Lawrence Fuchs's quotation on pp. 136–37 is from *The American Kaleidoscope,* p. 492.

The Myrdal quotation on p. 137 is from *An American Dilemma,* p. 50.

Richard Alba's quotation on p. 138 is from his book *Ethnic Identity: The Transformation of White America.* See the discussion in Andrew Hacker's article "Trans-National America," *The New York Review of Books,* November 22, 1990.

The 1996 survey of Hispanic parents on p. 138 was conducted by Market Development, Inc., *The Importance of Learning English,* released by the Center for Equal Opportunity, September 5, 1996.

PEN's Latino Literature Festival on p. 138 was reported by Jack Agueros, "No More 'Barrio-ization': We Are American Writers," *PEN-Newsletter,* Fall 1996.

The passages on pp. 138–39 concerning Hispanic-Americans and historical leaders are from Lawrence Fuchs's *The American Kaleidoscope,* p. 261.

Andrew Hacker's quotation on p. 139 is from *New York Newsday,* January 4, 1994.

The quotation on p. 141 from John Higham is from "History in the Culture Wars," Organization of American Historians *Newsletter,* May 1997; the quotation from Patricia Nelson Limerick is from her 1997 presidential address to the American Studies Association.

Herbert Croly's quotations on p. 141 are from his book *The Promise of American Life* (New York, 1909), pp. 139, 194. Croly was talking about class, not ethnic, divisions—indeed, he rather believed in the inferiority of blacks—but his general point remains sound.

The Orlando Patterson quotations on pp. 142–43 and 144 are from "White Man, Black Man" (with Chris Winship), *New York Times,* May 3, 1992, and "Race, Gender and Liberal Fallacies," *New York Times,* October 20, 1991.

The James Baldwin quotation on p. 143 is from his essay "The Discovery of What It Means to Be an American," quoted by Henry Louis Gates, Jr., *Nation,* July 15/22, 1991.

The Tocqueville quotation on p. 144 is from *The Old Regime and the French Revolution,* Part Three, chap. 4.

Diane Ravitch's quotation on p. 144 is from her article "Multiculturalism," p. 339.

EPILOGUE

William Raspberry's comment on p. 151 is from *The Washington Post,* September 4, 1991.

The quotation from Eric Hobsbawm on p. 152 is from "Identity Politics and the Left," *New Left Review,* May–June 1996.

The Todd Gitlin quotations on pp. 152–53 are from Gitlin, *The Twilight of Common Dreams* (New York, 1995), pp. 230, 84.

The Holmes quotation on p. 154 is from *Schenck* v. *United States,* 249 U.S. 47, 52 (1919); the Brandeis quotation is from *Whitney* v. *California,* 274 U.S. 357, 375.

The Holmes quotation on p. 154 is from *United States* v. *Schwimmer,* 279 U.S. 644, 655 (1929).

The Jackson quotation on p. 155 is from *West Virginia State Board of Education* v. *Barnette,* 319 U.S. 624, 642.

The Brennan quotation on p. 156 is from *Texas* v. *Johnson,* 491 U.S. 397, 414.

The quotation on p. 156 from Henry Louis Gates, Jr., is from his article, "Let Them Talk," *New Republic,* September 20, 1993.

The Kathryn Abrams quotations on p. 157 are from "Creeping Absolutism and Moral Impoverishment: The Case for Limits on Free Expression" in American Council of Learned Societies, Occasional Paper No. 22, *The Limits of Expression in American Intellectual Life* (New York, 1993), pp. 1, 3.

The quotation from the United Nations Convention on p. 158 is from Rodney A. Smolla, *Free Speech in an Open Society* (New York, 1992), p. 356.

Catherine MacKinnon's quotation on p. 159 is from her book *Only Words* (1993) and is discussed in Ronald Dworkin, "Women and Pornography," *New York Review of Books,* October 21, 1993, and Bernard Williams, "Drawing Lines," *London Review of Books,* May 12, 1994.

The letter quoted on p. 160 attacking Henry Louis Gates, Jr., appeared in the *Chronicle of Higher Education,* December 6, 1996.

The Bernard Shaw quotation on p. 160 is from *Annajanska* (1919).

For the decision of the Canadian Supreme Court in *Regina* v. *Butler,* quoted on p. 160, see National Coalition Against Censorship, *Censorship News,* Issue 4, 1993.

The Charles Lawrence quotations on p. 161 are from his article "Acknowledging the Victim's Cry," *Academe,* November–December 1990.

The Gates quotation on pp. 161–62 is from "Let Them Talk."

The Norman Corwin quotation on p. 162 is from John McDonough, "The Bill of Rights at 200," *The Wall Street Journal,* December 13, 1992.

Louis Menand's aphorism on p. 163 comes from his article "The Culture Wars," *New York Review of Books,* October 6, 1994.

Mr. Dooley's aphorism on p. 165 is from [Finley Peter Dunne], *Mr. Dooley's Philosophy* (New York, 1900), 258.

The Tocqueville quotation on p. 165 is from *Democracy in America,* II, Second Book, chap. vii.

Index

☆ ☆ ☆ ☆

199